Roadside With THE RT

Jim Blake

Visions International Entertainment Ltd

Two rogue RTs were allocated to Clapton Garage in May 1976 to cover RM shortages and used on the busy 38. On 6th July 1976, one of them, RT1161 (CT) crosses Islington "Angel" junction, with my former driver Bert Barlow at the wheel. Sadly, Bert passed away in 2007 having later worked at Abbey Wood and Plumstead Garages.

Roadside With THE RT

Published by Visions International Entertainment Limited

ISBN: 978-0-9931735-2-3

And after all that legal stuff, we hope you enjoy it.

Visions International Entertainment Limited
22, The Chase
Boreham, Essex, CM3 3DY
e-mail: deltic15@aol.com

For details of other bus and transport-related products, please visit the Visions web site:
http://www.visionsinternational.biz

CONTENTS

PUBLISHER'S NOTE

Welcome to our new 'Roadside Series'. I have long wanted to do a series of books featuring the various bus types that have, or continue to operate in London. One thing 'The Roadside' series isn't, is a definitive history, that's been done!

The idea is to give an overview of the day to day operations with photos that also bring back memories of life when the buses were operating. It might be through the milkman delivering his bottles or a store/pub that no longer exists, but it is memories, nostalgia, a time to float back to the days of your youth, the 'Good Old Days'.

The first volume features the RTs during the '60s & '70s. I was absolutely delighted that Jim Blake agreed to compile it, he has been a real joy to work with. Jim has created a collection of over 300 photographs which perfectly hit the remit for the series. The buses are fascinating but there is plenty of other interest in most of the photos, look beyond the bus! In addition, each is captioned with a wealth of historical information.

Each section has a theme and Jim uses them to take us on a tour through London during the days of the mighty RT. It has been a real pleasure putting this book together and I hope you enjoy it as much as we do.

KEN CARR
Boreham
May 2017

INTRODUCTION

Seventy Years ago, in May 1947, the first post-war London Transport RT-class buses entered service. The type had originally been introduced immediately before the outbreak of World War Two, owing to which production had to be suspended after only 150 of the class, in addition to the prototype, had been built.

Acute shortages of manpower and materials delayed resumption of production until almost two years after the war had ended, but the resulting vehicles embodied many improved features, some of which were a direct result of wartime advances in technology.

The task of the new buses was a daunting one, to replace all pre-war buses, along with non-standard types delivered during the war and immediately after it, together with replacing London's last remaining trams.

However, about a thousand of the older buses had to soldier on, mostly south of the Thames, since the war had thwarted their intended replacement by trolleybuses. So pressing was the need for the new buses, that their chassis manufacturer, A.E.C. based at Southall, was unable to meet the demand - about 7,000 buses in all - thus London Transport also had to purchase a quantity of Leyland Titan PD2's. Their chassis were subsequently adapted to become the 1,631-strong RTL class, to carry bodies that were basically interchangeable with those on RT chassis at overhaul.

Leyland also bodied 500 of these buses themselves, with bodies resembling RTs, but 8ft wide as opposed to the 7ft 6in width then standard for the rest of the fleet. These were the RTWs. All this left a total of 4,674 post-war RTs, which were delivered between the spring of 1947 and the end of 1954.

Unlike the original batch built between 1939 and 1942, which London Transport bodied themselves, contracts for bodying this vast fleet were let to Park Royal (who also bodied about two thirds of the RTL class) and Weymann for the majority of the buses, perhaps because both entities were based within London Transport's area, but 350 bodies were built by the Saunders Engineering & Shipyard Company on the island of Anglesey and a further 120 were built by Cravens of Sheffield. The latter were non-standard, having five-bay bodies instead of the standard four, and all were withdrawn in 1956/57. Except for the latter, all RT bus bodies were interchangeable on overhaul.

This speeded up the overhaul process, which was one of the main ideas for the buses. These were carried out in the huge Aldenham Overhaul Works from which newly-overhauled buses emerged as good as new, originally every three or four years.

Over the years many books have appeared featuring London's RTs - which were an iconic symbol of London for best part of forty years before the Routemasters superseded them - this one takes a look at them in their working environment. Instead of merely showing the buses themselves, for example with a boring standard three-quarter offside view in which nothing but the actual bus is seen - I have attempted to select views from my archives that show the environment they worked in. For example, a railway bridge or a British Railways or Underground station makes a nice background to a picture of a bus, as does a traditional English pub or a church.

Pictures may also show other road vehicles of bygone years, buildings that no longer exist and also the fashions of the time. It also makes a nice shot seeing an RT climbing a steep hill, or storming across the fields, and forests and through towns which made up the former London Transport area. I have divided the pictures into individual themes on this basis. All of the photographs used are my own. Many have not been published before, and if they have, it was a long time ago and whatever books or magazines they appeared in are long since out of print!

Incidentally, the codes shown in brackets after the fleet numbers of buses shown in this book are their London Transport garage codes, which are listed on page 114.

I must put on record my thanks to Ken Carr for encouraging me to put this collection together (not to mention for publishing it!), to Colin Clarke for scanning my entire negative collection from which my pictures are taken and also to the P.S.V. Circle and the London Omnibus Traction Society whose records enabled me to trace, and then chase, RTs in the 1960s and 1970s. Thanks are also due to my old friends John Gascoine and Terry Handorff who used to supply me with London Transport's overhaul programmes and variation sheets which often helped me keep one or more steps ahead of the enthusiasts' societies!

I hope readers will find this collection of photographs entertaining and different, for if they do, there's lots, lots more where they came from of other London Transport bus types in the period covered!

Finally, I would like to dedicate this book to my three grandchildren, Gracie and Freddie Denham and Oscar Blake McLellan.

JIM BLAKE
Palmers Green
May 2017

Main Cover Photo: On 26th October 1976, RT2775 (AD) substitutes for an RM on route 298A, but erroneously shows a route 298 number in its main blind box! It is seen at Palmers Green Triangle, where the idiot in the car on the right has obstructed the bus stop, causing the RT to pick up and set down passengers in the middle of the road. This RT had travelled to the United States in 1952 promoting Britain, and always kept its original body. It is now preserved.

Bottom Left Cover Photo: On 11th June 1976, RT2157 (LH) appears to have been abandoned in the street when standing at Tadworth Station on a short working of the 406, at the time officially RMC-operated. The car on the right, however, is obstructing its stand. This poor RT still exists, but is imprisoned in a yard in Camden Town in use as an estate agent's office!

Bottom Right Cover Photo: On 28th July 1976, RT2964 (AR), one of three allocated to Tottenham Garage to cover for ailing RMs at the time, is heading home in York Road, Waterloo outside County Hall. Behind it is the footbridge to the monstrous County Hall Island Block, now thankfully demolished!

PUBS

Many pubs in an around London were used as bus termini for many years. One of the most famous was The Royal Forest Hotel at Chingford, where they occupied its forecourt flanking Rangers Road. On 21st August 1968, a couple of weeks before the terminus was abandoned, RT2061 (AD) on the 102, RT4085 (T) on the 38 accompany rogue RTL502 (WH) on the 249 and another RT on the 179. The first stage of LT's Reshaping Plan on 7th September 1968 saw the terminus relocated to a new bus station adjacent to Chingford railway station, as well as the withdrawal of route 249 and the 38's cut back to Walthamstow. I have organised gatherings of vintage buses at this pub to re-create the old terminus since 1988.

Saunders roofbox-bodied RT2414 (T) is bound for the 38's new eastern terminus on 5th October 1968. It's passing The Mildmay Tavern in Balls Pond Road, a well-known North London pub, where in 1964, the Honeycombs pop group were "discovered". They went on to record "Have I The Right", which was the last No.1 hit scored by the eccentric independent record producer Joe Meek in his nearby Holloway Road studio.

On 29th May 1971, RT2020 (L) stands at the Abridge, Blue Boar terminus of Loughton circular route 167A. This route had been introduced upon "Reshaping" and had to be RT-operated as this stand was not suitable for One Person Operated (O.P.O) buses. For many years, this had been the terminus of route 10, running all the way from Central London. The 167A was withdrawn in April 1976, replaced by an extension of O.P.O. route 235 which continued to Theydon Bois, where the bigger MBs operating it could safely turn round.

Another London Transport outpost in South East Essex was Lambourne End, where The Beehive pub was used as a terminus. RT2780 (U) is reversing there on the Sunday 150A on 4th July 1971. This route was withdrawn three weeks later, but the 150 continued to serve this terminus until October 1977. Later renamed The Camelot, the pub is now The Beehive again, but the RTs that served it are a distant memory!

The Boston Arms opposite Tufnell Park Station is typical of the many Victorian "gin palaces" in this part of North London. On 12th July 1972, RT4021 (HT) passes it on its way to Waterloo on the recently revived route 4, having just set off from its nearby garage. This RT is one of several that had recently been recertified and repainted for a further three years' service. They had to be retained owing to the failure of the new MB, SM and DM-types meant to replace them.

Above: RT4292 (SW) substitutes for an RM on route 2 on 14th September 1973, and passes The Thurlow Arms, West Norwood. This was once a tram terminus for such routes as the 33, and the buses that replaced them used its forecourt for a few years.

Left: Country Area routes terminated at pubs, too. On 6th November 1975, RT2779 (GR) stands beneath the trees at The Black Lion, Shenley. It is one of several RTs retained at Garston garage for RML cover on routes such as the 311. At this time there was a severe spares shortage which kept many of them off the road, some never to run again. The RT also has an RM side blind in its via box.

On 9th April 1976, just a fortnight before route 247 succumbed to BLs and O.P.O., North Street's RT3697 passes The Thatchers Arms, Warley The route was later extended from Collier Row to replace the 250 and run all the way from Brentwood to Epping via Romford!

On a boiling hot 8th June 1976 RT2029 (SP) on route 51A escorts RT2554 (SP) on sister route 51 past Ye Olde Black Horse, Halfway Street. Both are working the routes' rush hour extension from Woolwich to Charlton Station. The 51's RTs would be replaced by RMs three days later, with the 51A following in January 1977. Their use on these routes would, however, be short-lived. The 51 was converted to DMS in May that year and the 51A withdrawn.

Kingston based RT1139 works one of the 71's odd rush hour journeys along Ham Street on 18th May 1977, passing between The Brewery Tap, a Watney's house, and The Old Green Man, a Courage one. Are these two pubs still thriving in this pleasant riverside village forty years later? Meanwhile, route 71 converted to RM early in 1978.

On 9th July 1978, last Sunday of RT operation on route 140, RT4772 (HD) passes The Red Lion in Harlington - an area threatened by plans to build a third runway at Heathrow Airport, to where the bus is heading. The Routemaster heading in the other direction is a Hendon RML on their small Sunday allocation. RMs would take over the 140's daily Harrow Weald allocation the following Saturday - some sixteen years after originally intended!

BRIDGES

London buses cross many bridges, few more famous than London Bridge itself! On 4th December 1967, as work to rebuild it begins, Saunders-bodied RT1656 (Q) heads south on the long route 35 from Chingford to Clapham Common. Note the dock cranes on the right, in what was still called the Pool of London at the time. Route 35 would be cut back to Hackney on 7th September 1968 and converted to RM.

Having just passed beneath the London Tilbury & Southend main line and District Line at Upminster Bridge Station on 29th June 1968, RT3502 (GY) has a good load of passengers on board. Route 370 would later be operated by downgraded RMC and RCL-class ex-Green Line coaches and today is one of a few former Country Area routes that still exist as part of the London Buses system.

On 23rd October 1969, a large merchant ship can be observed to the right of RT3718 (PR) which has just crossed Millwall Lock Bridge on the Isle Of Dogs loop route 56. The docks were then still, just about, in use, but the 56 was withdrawn two days later, replaced by an extension of the 277 (which the RT going in the other direction is working).

Tower Bridge is the most iconic bridge that London buses cross. On 3rd January 1970, RT815 (Q) has just safely negotiated its bascules - like the famous RT that had to jump between them when they were raised as it was crossing back in 1952. Three weeks after this photo was taken route 42 converted to MB O.P.O. Cranes in the docks are still in evidence on the left, but where are the crowds of tourists seen here in the 21st Century?

In complete contrast to Tower Bridge was the railway bridge across Addiscombe Road at Bingham Road Station. This was just high enough to accommodate an RT passing beneath, as shown by RT1533 (TC) on 19th September 1970. However, it was too low for an RM to pass under safely, thus the section of route 12 south of Norwood Junction was withdrawn and replaced by single-deck (originally SMS) route 12A in January 1972. Subsequently, the Southern Region branch using the bridge was closed, with Croydon Tramlink later taking over part of it, but using a level crossing at this point rather than a bridge!

A very picturesque little bridge is that crossing between Carshalton Ponds. Also on 19th September 1970, RT4474 (AL) crosses it on the southern section of weekend route 77B. By coincidence, both the 12 and the 77B (also the weekday 77) usually had their southern sections worked separately to their main in-town sections, and also had special three-line via blinds for them, as may be seen.

This massive 1930s concrete structure on Chingford side of Lea Valley Viaduct was later demolished when the road was widened. There is hardly any traffic on the North Circular Road as RT3467 (AD) heads east on the 34 in the evening of 6th October 1971! Superstores instead of factories flank the road here today.

On a short working of route 44 to Vauxhall, RT2327 (WD) passes beneath the Kent Coast main line beside Battersea Dogs Home on 13th May 1972, just over a month before this route converted to the awful DMS type. Cats are also housed at this home for strays nowadays!

Crossing another Southern Region main line, this time above that to Brighton at Lower Addisombe Road, East Croydon, RT924 (TH) has just passed one of its stablemates on route 197A on 1st September 1972. This route had been introduced two years previously and converted to DMS in May 1973.

For many years, route 101 was one of London's busiest, serving as it did the Royal Docks complex between Beckton and North Woolwich. But those days were already past on 2/10/72, when RT1390 (U) is seen crossing the King George V Dock swingbridge. RM's replaced RTs on this route at the end of the month.

RT2629 (SW) unusually susbstitutes for an RM on route 2B on 5th April 1973, amid the desolation caused by Vauxhall Cross roadworks. It passes beneath the footbridge for pedestrians over the south side of Vauxhall Bridge, which itself crosses the Thames. For several years in the 1980s, I would be co-owner of RT2629, then preserved and used for outings for the North London Transport Society. Where is it today?

Route 403 was the last major Country route to be RT operated. On 27th April 1973, RT3115 and RT3478 (both CM) pass on the railway bridge taking Waddon Road above the Southern Region line between West Croydon and Sutton.

On 18th September 1973, RT2164 (TL) passes beneath the Southern Region main line to Tonbridge and the South Coast just south of Orpington Station on route 94. Just under five years later it would be the last RT-operated route in South London, shared by Bromley and Catford Garages.

Also on 18th September 1973, RT574 (SP) passes beneath another Southern Region bridge - this time at Sidcup Station - as a unit of B.R. Standard S.R. 4-EPB stock crosses. This RT was one of the very last to have a full Aldenham overhaul (in January 1970), its stock number having been on "Works Float" since 1955! Route 228 would convert to RM in May 1977.

Upon route 277's DMS conversion in January 1974, it had to be rerouted away from the Isle of Dogs since some of the dock swingbridges there were too narrow for DMSs to pass. Thus route 277A was introduced with RTs covering that routeing, and effectively reviving the old 56, though at times the route continued to Hackney Station. On 23rd February 1974, RT4069 passes beneath the bridge carrying the London, Tilbury & Southend main line across Burdett Road. On the left is the bricked-up booking office to the station here, that was closed as a result of bomb damage during the 1940 Blitz.

On 16th July 1974, RT626 (SV) passes beneath the Great Northern main line at Little Wymondley, south of Hitchin: Restricted bridge height here (officially 13ft 9ins, as the sign shows) enforced RT working, as it was far too low for the ANs that had replaced most RTs at Stevenage in the autumn of 1972. Eventually, such journeys as ran beneath the bridge were converted to single-deck working.

A very battered RT2052 (NX) passes beneath the railway bridge in Rotherhithe New Road on 24th November 1974 on route 1, two months before its conversion to RM. This bridge housed the original Spa Road & South Bermondsey Station on the South Eastern & Chatham main line, closed in 1915. Much of its infrastructure still existed when the lines above were realigned a century later to improve the track layout.

In the same area as the previous picture, RT2166 (TB) passes beneath the bridge at Deptford Stationon 24th January 1975. Route 47 converted to RM two days later, and has been diverted away from this busy High Street and its market along nearby Deptford Church Street in more recent times.

Bushey Arches, just south of Watford town centre, carried the West Coast main line above many bus routes serving the town. On 30th April 1975, RT3607 (HH) passes beneath them on the long 301 route, running all the way to Aylesbury, though this journey is turning short at Tring Garage.

On the East Coast (Great Northern) main line, the bridge carrying Oakleigh Road above it had to replaced to allow the overhead electrification of suburban services. A Bailey bridge was erected while work progresses; on 10th July 1975, RT3467 crosses it, still working route 34 which by now has been rerouted to Leytonstone rather than Leyton. An RF on route 251 follows.

A bridge of a different kind is being built in Wood Green on 22nd May 1976, to connect the two halves of the new Shopping City either side of the High Road. Until its closure in 1963, the Great Eastern branch line to Palace Gates had crossed the road here at almost the same point. Here, RT4125 (AD) susbstitutes for an RM on route 298.

A short tunnel takes the Sevenoaks Road beneath the Southern Region main line south of Orpington. On 8th June 1976, RT1138 (SP) has just passed beneath it on route 51A bound for Green Street Green. This route retained RTs until January 1977, when it gained RMs - only to be withdrawn four months later!

On 18th June 1976 a very careworn RT2052 (TH) turns from Blackfriars Bridge onto Victoria Embankment on route 109, some three months before RTs were finally replaced on this tram replacement route after 25 years. Behind the RT is Blackfriars Railway Bridge, now very much altered with the station stretching right across the Thames with entrances both sides of the river.

Working local route 261 on 16th May 1977, RT3928 (AD) passes beneath the impressive Waterfall Road viaduct, which carries the Piccadilly Line between Arnos Grove and Southgate Stations. Graffiti on the bridge abutment reflects the political mood of the time - the National Front had held a march on the previous St. George's Day through this predominantly Jewish area, causing outrage. The 261 converted to DMS in April 1978 and no longer exists today.

RT816 (WW), whose bald roof confirms it has not been overhauled since January 1964, has just passed beneath the Enfield and Cheshunt local lines at Silver Street Station, Edmonton on 23rd August 1977. It is on a short working to New Southgate. A fortnight or so later route 34 converted to DMS operation. On many occasions, the dipped road under this bridge has flooded at times of heavy rain, sometimes submerging buses up to their waists!

STATIONS

Many London bus routes serve Underground or main line railway stations, and on 6th July 1968 Woolwich Arsenal Station still sports a Southern Railway name-board as RT4081 (AM) passes on the long route 122, on its way from Bexleyheath to Crystal Palace! This busy station has subsequently been linked to the Docklands Light Railway and Elizabeth Line (Crossrail) systems.

Offside loading like this would be a Health & Safety nightmare today, but on 21st August 1968 it wasn't a problem for these shoppers boarding Saunders-bodied RT4637 (AD) at Southgate Station! This tube station, opened for the Piccadilly Line extension to Cockfosters in 1932 and is one of Chas Holden's masterpieces. Route 29A was renumbered 298A upon "Reshaping" on 7th September 1968.

Underneath the arches on 21st September 1968, RT1982 (PR) stands at the terminus of route 82, which ran through the Rotherhithe Tunnel to Surrey Docks Station. This route had converted from RTL a fortnight before, but RTs worked it only for a further five weeks, as it was withdrawn on 26th October 1968. This LT&S Line station has subsequently been renamed Limehouse and is also served by the DLR today.

On 16th March 1969, RT2809 (SV) is one of two standing at the old Stevenage Station, which was north of Stevenage Old Town. Despite Stevenage New Town growing rapidly in the 1950s and 1960s, the station was not resited adjacent to its town centre until 1973, meaning that buses on New Town services like the 809 had to travel through the Old Town to connect with trains. The adverts on the right for the 1950s Chris Barber Jazz Band could almost fool readers into thinking this picture was taken in that decade, but the 809 was not introduced until the 1960s!

Greenford Station, on the post-war Central Line extension to West Ruislip, is unusual with escalators going UP to its platforms on bridge over Oldfield Lane! It forms a nice backdrop to this view of RT4705 (HW) loading up on route 92 on 26th May 1970. This route converted to SMS O.P.O. a year later.

At Oakwood Station, RT2582 (FY) loads up Saturday route 125A on 19th December 1970. This route, which covered the 298A between here and Southgate Station on Saturdays, was withdrawn three weeks later when the parent 125 converted to SMS. A group of 1950s and 1960s cars occupy the station car park, overshadowed by the LT bullseye!

RT2408 (AV) on a short working of the 203 on 15th April 1971, passing Hounslow West, another Charles Holden station then at the western extremity of the Piccadilly Line. It was later rebuilt when the line was extended to Heathrow Airport. By then, the 203 had long since been converted to O.P.O.

By 29th May 1971, the forecourt of Enfield Chase Station on the Great Northern Hertford Loop had become the Saturday terminus of route 107A, which had continued to Edgware and Queensbury at weekends until the parent 107 lost RTs in July 1970. RT1131 (E) will have quite a short journey to Enfield Lock, therefore! The 107A was withdrawn in September 1972

A host of semaphore signals and the rusting girders of uncompleted Northern Line extension platforms and facade shortly before their demolition form the backdrop to RT1816 (HT) at the Finsbury Park Station terminus of route 4 on 1st July 1972. A patch is still visible below the offside sidelight where the L plate had been when RT was a trainer!

On 12th July 1972, RT4515 (GR) calls at Croxley Station, on the Metropolitan Line's Watford branch, shortly before route 321 (or is it 321A?) converted to AN O.P.O. The RT was one of thirty-four sold back to London Transport by London Country a few weeks later to help cover shortages of the time. The station has typical 1920s Metropolitan Railway architecture.

On 14th July 1972 Palmers Green's RT3334 passes East Finchley Station on its way to Chingford on route 102. This Chas Holden masterpiece, complete with the sculpture of an archer pointing his arrow towards Central London, was never fully used for its intended purpose of sending tube trains to that area. Electrification of the L.N.E.R. branch via Highgate and Crouch End to Finsbury Park, and its link to the Northern City Line and Moorgate was put on hold as a result of World War Two and abandoned after it, despite much work having been completed for it - a mere £3m's worth at 1939 values in fact was wasted on the uncompleted Northern Line extensions! Meanwhile, route 102 converted to RM early in 1978.

Route 273 was introduced in November 1968, replacing parts of routes 97 and 211, then extended in 1972 replacing parts of the 98A. Shortly after that, on 20th July 1972, RT3392 (HW) crosses the bridge at Hillingdon Station on its circuitous journey to Ealing. At this time, the station here was very much its original self, little more than a halt. It was substantially rebuilt in the 1990s.

On 16th October 1972, rush hour commuters do not look very happy waiting for their buses at London Bridge Station, where there is a complete lack of shelter! RT4403 (NX) loads up for the long journey to Sidcup Garage, in an area served by trains from this station anyway! A covered bus station was built a few years later and has since itself been demolished and resited. Route 21 converted to RM in February 1975.

Ploughing through the rain beneath the bridge at Penge West Station on 6th March 1973, four days before Elmers End's share of the 12 converted to RM. RT2706 (ED) passes below a splendid B.R. Southern Region sign advertising the station, which is today part of the London Overground network.

Below: Hayes Station sports current British Rail signage. On 23rd September 1973, RT1329 (SP) stands outside on one of the odd Sunday afternoon journeys that were extended there on route 51 from Farnborough. Peculiarly, other journeys were extended via a different routeing to Bromley Garage.

Below: With a rather vague destination saying merely "Watford", RT3752 (GR) calls at Watford Junction Station on 20th June 1974. This was the last London Country RT to receive a full Aldenham overhaul (in the spring of 1972), and received a lighter shade of green paint than usual, though with yellow fleet number and name. The station sports B.R., L.T. and National Express emblems - being an interchange for coaches operated by the latter entity, too. Today, the Bakerloo Line no longer serves it, but local trains are operated by London Overground instead.

At Epping Station, eastern extremity of the main Central Line from Central London, on 26th September 1974 RT3816 (HA) is on one of the 339's double-runs through Epping, whilst a badly blinded RT2504 (HA) is about to set out to distant Bishops Stortford. In recent years, RTs have worked shortened versions of both routes in connection with the Epping Ongar heritage railway and the North Weald Bus Rally.

Thanks to an idiot parking his car (just visible on the left) in the bus stop, passengers have to board in the road. The lady boarding RT3628 (HD) on route 140 outside Burnt Oak Station on 30th December 1974 shows just what a high step it is onto an RT's platform when the bus cannot pull into the kerb. The RT has recently been repainted and recertified for another three years' service at exactly the time when the last was due to have been withdrawn! It did last that long, and spent a further year as a trainer.

With a Southern Region 4CIG unit speeding across the bridge above at Norbury Station, RT3232 (BN) passes one of its fellows on route 109 on 21st May 1976, shortly before the long-protracted conversion of this busy route to RM began. This RT had started life as a Green Line coach, was then downgraded to Country Bus status and passed to London Country. It was one of the thirty-four sold back to LT in 1972, and has subsequently been preserved and restored to original livery.

LEVEL CROSSINGS

On one of the relatively few level crossings that London buses cross, RT948 (E) crosses the tracks of the Lea Valley line at Enfield Lock Station on 11th July 1970. The driver has already changed his blind to show Edgware Station, the other end of a long journey across the top of the Central Area. The following week, the trip would take even longer when MBs replaced the RTs!

On the other side of London, RT4774 (AV) crosses the third-rail Southern Region tracks at Hampton Station on the short-lived route 211, which lasted only from the summer of 1969 to April 1971. Operated by RFs on Mondays to Fridays and RTs on Saturdays, it had replaced part of route 111 when that converted to MB O.P.O.

On 13th July 1972, RT3378 (GR) crosses the single-track Watford Junction - St. Albans Abbey branch line at Watford North Station. This is a former red RT that, in common with many others, was overhauled in 1963/64 with early RT3/1 bodies in green livery to replace all roofbox RTs in the Country Area. New ANs replaced RTs on this route the next day.

RT2922 (AP) has just bounced over the level crossing at Dagenham Dock Station on one of route 139's journeys to the dock itself on 23rd September 1972. Route 148 also served these points, and both routes converted to DMS in July 1977. Neither route exists in this area today; the area itself is much changed, too.

An oddity on Good Friday 28th March 1975 is RT2296 (AW) working Sunday-only route 180A, which was never scheduled for RT operation, always RMs in the six years (1972-1978) it ran. It is on the level crossing at Abbey Wood Station, which will soon be replaced by a bridge then under construction to improve access to the new Thamesmead Estate nearby.

Back in the former Country Area, RT3252 (WR) crosses other Southern Region line at Thorpe near Staines, as an RML heads the other way on 11th July 1975. The RT is one of several kept on at various London Country garages to cover for RMLs off the road at the time due to an acute shortage of spare parts.

Brimsdown is another station on the Lea Valley line with a level crossing. This one has continental-style barriers, which are open for RT4436 (E) to cross on 27th August 1975 on weekday route 135A. This served the Lockfield Avenue Industrial Estate on the other side of the tracks from Brimsdown proper. The route was renumbered 135 (following the closure of the power station that route served) two years later, but no longer exists today. A retail park now occupies the land where once industry flourished in this area.

One of the three London Country RTs which were adorned in full National Bus Company livery in the spring of 1977, RT1018 (CM), has just crossed the tracks at Whyteleafe Station on the Caterham branch on 1st June 1977. Its otherwise smart appearance is marred by the clumsy and torn blinds. Service use of the three RTs (the others were RT604 and RT3461) in this livery was short-lived, though they were retained for a few years as trainers and all were subsequently preserved.

CHURCHES

Churches often provide an imposing backdrop to pictures of buses, a good example being St. Peter's in St. Albans. RT650 (SA) passes it on 28th September 1968 working local route 358. This is one of a number of RTs that were painted in Green Line livery in 1960 for rush hour and bank holiday extras on busy coach routes. They could be distinguished from those RTs originally delivered as Green Line coaches by only having a painted Green Line bullseye between decks, rather than a metal raised one bolted to the panels.

Epping Church is another imposing edifice. Next day, a very wet 29th September 1968, RT577 (HA) calls there on the 339's double-run to serve Epping town and station. It was the lowest-numbered post-war green RT, another that had been overhauled green ex-red. Otherwise, the first one was RT597. This means that other low-numbered green RTs in preservation today, for instance RT593, are false: they should be red!

On 19th September 1970, RT1916 (TH) negotiates the sharp turn outside St. Leonard's church, Streatham on the circuitous 115B, a Sunday version of the equally roundabout 115. There is a second church on the other side of the road and it would be interesting to see if both are still in use today, bearing in mind the apparent drop in Christian worship nowadays. Meanwhile, this route was withdrawn a month later and the parent 115 converted to SMS at the beginning of 1971.

The sign for The Queen's Head pub obstructs this view of the Baptist Church in the village of Green Street Green as RT2598 (SP) begins its journey to Woolwich on 6th July 1971. Both the 51 and 51A would convert to RM for a few months before the latter was withdrawn in May 1977 and replaced by a re-routed 51, which gained O.P.O. DMSs at the same time.

St. Mary's Church in Upper Street is Islington's parish church, dating back originally to the 12th century and substantially enlarged in the 19th century. Apart from its spire, it was demolished during the Blitz in September 1940, and not reconstructed until 1956. On Christmas Day 1972, RT447 (HT) calls there. This was most unusual, since the 19 had converted to RM the previous August and few buses ran on Christmas Day. Now no London buses run at all on Christmas Day.

St. Paul's, Canonbury is not very far away from St. Mary's and this one survived the Blitz, only to be closed for worship in recent years. However, it is a listed building and is used for other community activities today. It forms a backdrop to RT3221 (PR) turning short into Dove Road to reach the Mildmay Park stand on 24th November 1973, some six weeks before the 277 converted to DMS.

Above: St. Clement Danes in the Strand is one of London's most famous churches, and was completely burnt out during the Blitz. Appropriately, following its rebuilding, it was adopted as the R.A.F. church, complete with a statue outside of "Bomber" Harris, who repaid Nazi Germany in kind! It is seen behind RT3868 (HT) which has just climbed up from Victoria Embankment on 28th May 1975, some two months before crew DMs replaced RTs on this tram replacement route. The lack of traffic along The Strand and into Aldwych is of note!

Left: Two churches which survived the wrath of the Luftwaffe form a backdrop to RT2116 (BK) at Holborn Circus heading into town on Night Bus route N95 early on the morning of 26th June 1975. Many other churches in the City were destroyed during the Blitz, particularly during the "second Great Fire of London" on 29th December 1940.

On 10th July 1975, RT994 (GR) pulls out of Elstree Road into the High Road by Bushey Parish Church. Many of the RMLs based at Garston for routes such as this, the 311 and 347 were kaput at this period due to a shortage of spares, obliging RTs to be used to cover for them - they even used their blinds, as can be seen! This blind arrangement would soon become common in the former Central Area for the same reason.

Working route 217B, the last new RT-operated route to be introduced (in April 1976), RT1572 (E) passes Waltham Abbey on 28th May 1977, some three months before this, and the 217, converted to DMS. The Abbey dates back to 610 A.D. and is reputed to be haunted!

One of last rogue RTs covering for RM shortages, RT1069 (HT), is at the Highbury Barn terminus of route 19 as autumn leaves fall on 11th November 1977. Christchurch, Highbury is behind the RT - this is Arsenal F.C.'s church, and also where I was Christened!

MARKET DAY

Since the very start of their operation, London buses have played an important role in taking shoppers to and from market. On 20th December 1967, Christmas shoppers vie for places aboard RTs in Islington High Street, having shopped at nearby Chapel Market. However, Saunders-bodied RT3187 (J) is going nowhere, having been unusually curtailed at this point. It is in fact working route 4A, the route-number 4 is incorrect, that route having been withdrawn at the end of 1966. The 4A was renumbered 4 in September 1971.

On a very wet Saturday, 30th March 1968, RT2163 (SA) on local route 343 calls at the busy St. Albans street market flanking St. Peter's Street. The many bus routes serving this busy market were all either RT or RF-operated at this time, but many of the local services converted to MBS early the following year.

Shoppers throng around Saunders-bodied RT1317 (HD) on 1st June 1968 outside South Harrow Station, which has a busy market beneath the railway arches. Another RT on route 140 brings up the rear. That route retained RTs for another ten years, but the 158 was withdrawn in October 1971. Its northern section, to Watford Junction, was replaced by the new 258, which still runs there today.

Enfield Town Market was very busy on Saturday 29th June 1968, as newly-overhauled RT2869 (E) calls on route 231 bound for Alexandra Park. The 231 was cut back to Turnpike Lane from this point upon Reshaping, then converted to SMS in September 1971 but still links the latter point with Enfield today. Note the side adverts resembling RM-style bus blinds.

It is also Market Day at Dartford Market Place on 6th July 1968 as RT872 (SJ) loads up with shoppers on the busy 477. This is another Country RT that was originally red. Note the "smoking" advert - something now strictly verboten on the buses! The advert for Guinness on the adjacent billboard is of note too - how long before adverts such as these are banned too on "Health and Safety" grounds?

Also on 6th July 1968, RT1140 (SJ) picks up shoppers at Bexleyheath Market Place. The 401 was odd in that its inner section, between Belvedere and Bexley was entirely within Greater London, but it then meandered all the way through the Kentish countryside to Sevenoaks. The RT is yet another "green ex-red".

Green RT3536 (GR) stands in for an RML on local route 346 on 13th July 1968, as it escorts a red RT on route 142 away from busy Watford Market. London bus routes 142 and 258 still serve the town today, but, for the most part, the many Country Area routes that did so fifty years or so ago are long gone.

Below: Romford Market is always busy, and on 29th May 1970 RT4381 (AP) is one of two RTs loading up with shoppers on St. Edward's Way, a road built to by-pass the market itself a few years beforehand. The 193 retained RTs until October 1976, though was cut back from Upminster to Hornchurch in July 1970. RTs working odd journeys on route 87 could still be seen in Romford until the very end in April 1979.

RT3668 (A) loads up on trolleybus replacement route 154 on 19th April 1973 in busy West Croydon - how will shoppers cope with the new DMSs on this route three weeks later? Croydon's trams now run here, beside the railway station now served by London Overground.

On 1st September 1977, rogue RT690 (WN) heads south along busy Wood Green High Road in place of a scheduled RM on route 29. The solitary Union Flag above it is a reminder of the Queen's Silver Jubilee celebrated a few months before. Many of the shops and market stalls along here were put out of business by the new Shopping City straddling the High Road, which was half-built at this time.

RT1654 (AM) passes through busy Woolwich Market Place on 15th April 1978, the last Saturday of RTs on 122. Tram tracks are still present under the RT's rear wheels, more than 25 years after London's last trams ran here! A DMS follows on route 122A, which had lost RTs in the summer of 1969.

Lewisham Bus Station, just around the corner from the street market and adjacent to the railway station, was opened shortly before the last RTs ran in South East London on route 94. RT2623 (TL) loads up with shoppers there on Saturday 25th August 1978, their penultimate day of operation. A new DMS completes the picture, but the 94 was converted to RM and then withdrawn four years later, never receiving them. Part of the space the bus station occupied was subsequently used for the terminus of the Docklands Light Railway extension to Lewisham.

SUNDAY SERVICE

Over the years, many bus routes worked to different destinations on Sundays, usually being extended to cover others, whilst there were also several Sunday-only routes. A good example was the 188A which covered the Archway Station to Holborn section of the 172 and the Holborn to Greenwich section of the 188. Holloway Road is deserted as RT1554 (J) passes the original Highbury & Islington tube station on 26th November 1967! The 188A was withdrawn in March 1971. Few routes have Sunday variations today.

Left: Route 90C was a Sunday variation of the 90 group of routes that covered the 90 from Staines to Richmond, and then continued via Chiswick Bridge to Hammersmith Metropolitan Line Station. A smart RT785 (AB) stands at the latter terminus on 2nd September 1968, its final day, which was in fact a late summer bank holiday Monday. New route 290, using RFs, replaced the Hammersmith to Richmond section of the route from Saturday 7th.

Below: Route 59 was perhaps THE epitome of Sunday-only routes for many years, running all the way from West Hampstead to the North Downs! This view however was taken on Easter Monday, 7th April 1969 - exactly ten years before the last RTs were withdrawn. RT4042 (TC), freshly overhauled "red ex-green", is an extra supplementing the usual RMLs used at this time. It has just crossed Westminster Bridge. My workplace for many years, London County Hall, is on the right.

On Sunday 19th December 1971, RT3964 (HT) passes Islington Green working the 19's Sunday extension beyond Tooting Bec, which replaced the 181 on Sundays between there and Streatham Garage. Its driver appears to be blinded by glaring winter sun! The statue in the background is of Sir Hugh Myddelton, who built the New River in the early part of the 17th century to bring fresh water to the City. This still runs nearby.

RT2145 (BK) on 3rd September 1972, exactly a year before the 169's conversion to DMS. The Sunday 169C followed the 169 from Barking to Barkingside, then the weekday 129 to Claybury Braodway, where it has just terminated. The flag on the bus stop shows "Alighting Point Only": buses picked up for the return journey around the corner. Needless to say this route has long since ceased to operate, along with all other suffixed routes in London.

A Routemaster on route 155's Sunday extension beyond its usual Wimbledon terminus to Hampton Court has let the side down by breaking down, adding to the Easter Monday holiday traffic on 23rd April 1973. RT344 (NB) is one of a number of the type supplementing the RMs that day and overtaking the stricken RM in Hampton Court Road.

For many years, routes 205 and 205A ran on Sundays only. Their joint service between Waltham Abbey and Flamstead End must have been disrupted on the last day they ran, 4th April 1976, for two to be seen together! Both routes ran entirely outside the Greater London area, despite being Central Area (red) bus routes. RT2268 (L) is nearest the camera.

In its last few years of RT operation, route 140 had a couple of journeys diverted off the main route between Hayes and Heathrow on Sundays to serve Cherry Lane Cemetery for the benefit of the bereaved visiting their loved ones' graves. On 23rd April 1978, RT2143 (HD) sets down a group of elderly ladies outside the cemetery gates. Although some RTs did have special blinds to denote the diversion via the cemetery, this one has not, and the driver has had to clip a handwritten note on his timecard and place it in the cab window!

MISHAPS & BREAKDOWN

Even in their final years, it was very unusual to see an RT being towed back to its garage after breaking down when in service. But this has happened to RT4172 (AL) on 29th October 1972, when it is being towed home to Merton Garage along Balham High Road by one of LT's Thames Trader recovery trucks. It had been working weekend route 77C.

Stored in the rear yard of Stonebridge Park Garage on 18th October 1970, Saunders-bodied RT1317 has suffered serious rear-end damage. This was apparently incurred when it was one of a number of withdrawn RTs on loan to the Road Research Laboratory in June. It went for scrap in November. This view clearly shows how Saunders-bodied RTs had their offside route number stencil-holders set back further than on other RTs.

In 1971 Kingston Coal Yard was being used as an overflow parking area for the nearby garage. Trainer RT857 has had a nasty rear-end accident and is awaiting disposal on 17th July 1971. It had come to grief in April, and also went for scrap shortly after this photo was taken. Its rear adverts are somewhat ironic! Interestingly, it was one of just two red RTs with RT3/1 bodies, which also still had cream waistbands, that survived by this time. The other one, RT801, lasted as a trainer until early 1976.

In the yard of Merton Garage itself, RT1597 (AL) has suffered damage to its cab area when seen on a murky 29th November 1975. Somewhat surprisingly, it was soon repaired - perhaps because of the vehicle shortages at that time - and remained in service until June 1976. It was later preserved, but sadly destroyed by arsonists a few years afterwards.

Inside Stevenage Garage on 28th May 1972, Country RT4036 (SV) has just received a nasty dent in its cab area. By this time, such relatively light damage was sufficient to condemn an RT, so it was sent to Hertford for store a few days later and sold for scrap in September 1972.

This very spectacular damage to RT2525 (AD) was caused by a heavy lorry jumping the lights at the junction of the new section of the North Circular Road, Sterling Way, and Silver Street in Edmonton, and striking the RT almost head on. Fortunately, its driver escaped serious injury, but the bus was written off, since it chassis was distorted by the impact as well as the damage to the body. Following a tow back to the garage, it awaits scrapping at Palmers Green Garage on 25th January 1976.

INDUSTRIAL AREA SPECIALS

A number of bus routes had special journeys extended to Industrial Estates, or operated specifically to serve them. An odd example was route 299, which usually ran from Southgate to South Mimms but had a single rush hour return journey extended to/from Borehamwood, Chester Road. RT4011 (PB) stands there on 23rd June 1971, shortly before the route converted to SMS.

Another oddity involved routes 62 and 247, which had rush hour journeys diverted off their normal route to serve the Hainault Industrial Estate. RT1562 (NS) is seen there on the latter on 12th July 1972. Its final blind reads: "Harold Hill Gooshays Drive via Fowler Road"!

The bus stop E-plate reads "54: Monday to Friday rush hours only" at route 54's Woolwich Industrial Estate terminus in Nathan Way, where RT1561 (TL) has arrived on 30th August 1972. A full timetable for the route is visible on the stop post. This was the only route to serve this industrial area before it was engulfed by the Thamesmead development.

Below: The conductor is apparently checking to see whether his driver has set RT965's blind correctly for the run to Barking Garage as it collects workmen from Creekmouth Power Station on 6th March 1973, shortly before route 23C's withdrawal. This was an irregular route that ran to suit the workers' shifts. It was replaced by certain journeys on the 62 extended to this desolate area. This area too has been redeveloped in recent times.

Below: A very complicated network of routes served the Stevenage Industrial Area, which was the other side of the tracks of the Great Northern main line to the New Town proper. In the last week of RT operation, RT603 (SV) loads up in Gunnels Wood Road on route 800A. Workings serving this area had the words "Industrial Area" printed beneath their number blinds, as shown here. Note also the standard LT tubular shelters and LT bus stop flags still in use nearly three years after the Country Area was split off.

RT1288 (PM) accompanies one of its fellows at Park Royal Trading Estate terminus on 20th March 1973, when route 12 was in the throes of a protracted conversion to RM operation. About half of the RT/RTL fleet, and all of the production Routemasters, were bodied here by Park Royal Vehicles, whose main offices may be glimpsed in the distance between the two RTs. Buses on routes 12, 220 and 226 had journeys extended here in rush hours at this time, when PRV were churning out the DMS class!

Dwarfed by one of the huge cooling towers serving Brimsdown Power Station, RT1989 (E) sets off on the135's almost circular route to Carterhatch on 27th August 1975. The route was extended here in rush hours to serve the power station, and was diverted to nearby Lockfield Avenue two years later after the power station closed. Today, a retail park occupies most of both areas.

Another very desolate industrial area served by London's buses was the Greenwich peninsular, south east of Blackwall Tunnel. Route 185 had journeys extended there to serve Delta Metal Works, from which terminus RT783 (WL) departs for home on the route's last day of RT operation, 11th May 1973. The Millennium Done was subsequently built on former industrial land near this location.

Very late in the RTs' working lives, in August 1976, route 120 was extended from Greenford Station into the Bridge Park Lyons Factory Estate. On 18th May 1977, RT2566 (HW) is within the estate, viewd from the other side of the Grand Union Canal which buses had to cross in order to regain the rest of the route, which finally lost RTs in January 1978.

Journeys on routes 139 and 148 ran into Dagenham Dock, from where RT2295 (NS) departs on 22nd July 1977, for the benefit of dock workers. Bonded warehouses here meant that public entry was controlled by a guard in the booth on the left. Both routes converted to DMS O.P.O. the next day.

SCHOOL DAYS

As well as catering for workers, London buses catered for scholars too, with a number of routes specially extended to serve schools and in some cases specifically running for schoolchildren, as is still the case today. On 5th March 1969, RT3462(NF) passes between The Sun and The Wheatsheaf pubs in Gravesend Overcliff on an afternoon trip to Dover Road Schools on local route 497. Shortly afterwards, scholars using this route had the dubious pleasure of riding on new MBSs instead!

The long route 54 had school journeys to Riddlesdown, from where RT524 (ED) sets off on a short working to its home garage on 14th July 1972. A sad indication of how life has changed since this picture was taken is that any bus enthusiasts photographing buses filled with schoolchildren today would probably be mistaken for paedophiles, or "dirty old men" as they were called back in 1972!

An odd extension serving Hampton Grammar School was that of the already long route 72 (East Acton - Hampton Court Station), which continued across Hampton Court Bridge into Hampton itself. On 20th July 1972, RT553 (R) turns from Broad Lane into Nightingale Road, Hampton on the approach to the school.

Above: In south-east London, route 94 was extended from Orpington alongside the 51 and 51A to Sidcup Station, also for the benefit of children attending nearby schools. Buses on this route, as well as short workings on the 51, 228 and 229, actually stood in Alma Road, where RT2812 (TL) is one of two shown arriving on the 94. However there are no schoolchildren to collect on 1st September 1972 as they are still on summer holiday! Evidently the buses still operated these journeys regardless!

Left: Route 77A, which ran from Kings Cross to Raynes Park, had a long extension for school journeys to Worcester Park Station. RT3056 (AL) is accompanied there by an Evening Standard mini-van and a black cab on 6th October 1972.

Several special routes ran for schools in the Watford area. Among them was the 318C, yet RT3636 (GR) seen loading up outside Queens School on 20th June 1974 has little indication of what route it is really working, other than a canopy blind showing 318! This is probably because RMLs and MBSs meant to operate these routes are out of action, and the RT which has had to fill the breach does not have suitable blinds!

A remarkable Central Area school operation in the mid-1970s was that of journeys on route 175A which served Ongar Comprehensive School out in the wilds of rural Essex! Buses actually ran into the school grounds, which RT4405 (NS) is seen leaving on 26th September 1974. The route served such villages as Stanford Rivers, Passingford Bridge and Stapleford Abbotts on its way to Romford. Needless to say, cuts to "out-county" London bus routes soon put paid to such workings!

The long 122 route (Bexleyheath - Crystal Palace) had school journeys which terminated off the main route at Eltham Green, and stood in Middle Park Avenue. Selfishly parked cars on this deviation caused such disruption to the service that it featured on the local TV news, and indeed RT1175 (AM) had trouble getting there on 5th November 1974. It loads up with schoolchildren as the clippie, complete with regulation Gibson ticket machine, looks on.

RT994 (GR) on 16th July 1975 outside Queens School, Watford, does have a blind display on this occasion, albeit a via blind from an RML and a canopy blind in the number box. It appears to be working route 346D!

TERMINUS

London's bus termini vary from small side-streets to major bus stations. One that has been in use and remained largely unchanged for well over a century is that in the middle of the roundabout at Muswell Hill Broadway, where RT2000 (MH) arrives on a 212 Express journey on 24th April 1968. Such journeys were introduced in 1954 as a poor substitute for the railway from Finsbury Park that closed in July that year, but should have become part of the Northern Line tube in 1940. The 212 was replaced in May 1969 by flat-fare route W7, which still serves the same termini today.

Left: A long-vanished terminus is that at Eltham, Well Hall Station, which RT666 (NX) leaves bound for Cannon Street on route 182 on 28th May 1968. Equipped with its own LT staff canteen, it was swept away along with the adjacent Southern Region station upon the extension of the M2 in the 1980s, and replaced along with Eltham Park Station by a new Eltham Station situated half-way between the two. Meanwhile, route 182 was withdrawn in June 1968. It was a tram replacement route that duplicated route 21 all the way from Eltham to Borough.

Below: A number of London Transport Country Area bus garages had bus stations adjoining them. A good example was Windsor, where on 1st June 1968, RT2878 (MA) awaits departure on the long 353 route to Berkhamsted. Another RT and a modernised Green Line RF accompany it. The garage and bus station here are now but a distant memory, too.

Framed by the platform canopy of another RT in front to shield me from the sun on 15th October 1968, Saunders-bodied RT3809 (PR) is one of three standing at the Bromley-By-Bow terminus of Blackwall Tunnel route 108, which was in a typical East End back street. There were many such cases where frequent bus routes began and ended their journeys in residential streets. RTs replaced RTLs on the tunnel routes on 7th September 1968, but lasted only until 26th October 1968 when MBs replaced them in turn. This was due to the work undertaken to widen the Blackwall Tunnel. The roadway was filled in between the kerbs, thus reducing the height, between the roadway and roof, thus making it too low for double-deckers.

Below: In pouring rain on 25th October 1969, RT3140 (DG) is working local route 421 in Sevenoaks Bus Station. A number of such establishments existed in the Country Area and standard LT tubular shelters are much in evidence here.

There were two bus stations in Guildford, both shared by London Transport and local B.E.T. operator Aldershot & District. RT3116 (GF) is at the larger one at Onslow Street on 26th October 1969 working local route 408A. This was sometimes also operated by RLHs, one of which is in the background along with an A&D Dennis Loline and a GS. The latter is one that had been sold to independent operator Tillingbourne Valley, some of whose routes were also ex-London Transport.

At the Upminster, Hall Lane terminus of route 248, RT1716 (RD) passes RLH71 (RD) on route 193A, working its rush hour extension to Eastern Avenue on 18th September 1970. This was the last day of this route, which had only been introduced two months previously. Next day, it was withdrawn and the 248 converted to SMS and extended to Romford to cover it.

The forecourt of the George and Dragon pub at Farnborough was a bus terminus on the edge of the Central area for many years. On 9th August 19/71, RT2839 (SP) on the 51 and RT1797 (TB) on the 47 share it. The latter is working one of its route's many short workings to Lewisham, and correctly shows a via blind meant for these.

The long 47's in-town terminus was this on-street stand beside Shoreditch Church. The famous pioneering workers' flats at Arnold Circus form a backdrop. On the evening of 12th May 1972, four RTs are on the stand. The third one is a 78, but the others are all 47's, of which the leading one is RT233 (TL) about to run back to its home garage. It correctly shows a via blind for through journeys to Farnborough, which as may be seen differs from that shown in the previous picture.

Centre: Many termini on the edge of the Central Area were in the middle of nowhere, beyond the built-up area. Typical was route 87's traditional terminus at Rainham, White Post Corner, where RT1776 (BK) performs a three-point turn on 23rd September 1972. By now few journeys ran to this outpost, most turning at Abbey Wood Lane in a nearby residential area instead. This route 87 no longer exists today. Note the Post Office Telephones Morris Minor van, whose driver has been attending to the apparatus on the pole behind the RT.

Below: Route 21 also had short journeys from its outer terminus (at Sidcup Garage) to Lewisham, where several routes stood behind the cinema in Rennell Street. On 14th April 1973 careworn RT4164 (SP), complete with a via blind meant for through workings to Moorgate, arrives as passengers jump off the still-moving bus. This is something they could not do once routes converted to one-person-operation. The new Lewisham Bus Station replaced this terminus in the summer of 1978.

Many routes had short journeys mid-way along their routes, a good example being the Country route 339 which ran from Harlow to Warley via Epping. Several journeys turned from the Harlow end at Ongar, Two Brewers, where a battered RT1700 (HA) stands on 2nd June 1973. By a remarkable coincidence, this RT was later preserved and at the time of writing runs route 339 between Epping and Ongar in association with the heritage railway!

The Ford Motor Company's huge Dagenham works complex had its own bus station, to which several routes in the area were extended. RT4405 (NS) loads up there on route 175 on 22nd August 1973. By now, few of the workers used the buses, preferring to use cars they had probably helped build themselves. The RTs on this route were replaced by ex-British Airways RMAs during 1975/76, returning briefly in 1977 before normal RMs took over.

A number of bus routes terminated at Clapham Junction, which in the mid-1970s boasted four different stands! One was in Abyssinia Road, where two RTs acting as RM substitutions are found on 28th December 1973. Nearest the camera is RT693 (HT). Route 19 only gets as far south as Battersea Bridge nowadays.

Below: Another three-point reversal terminus on the London/Essex borders was at Noak Hill, Pentowan, where RT3534 (NS) backs into a farmyard to do a three-point turn on 13th April 1974. It too is an RM sub and by now, few journeys served this point. Most buses on the 174 terminated at Tees Drive, on the edge of the post-war L.C.C. Harold Hill Estate.

Left: The bus station at the rear of Turnpike Lane tube station was enlarged and roofed in 1967 in preparation for the Reshaping Plan route changes in the Wood Green area. On the evening of 29th November 1976, RT280 (WN), one of two RTs sent to assist RM shortages on route 141, has turned short there. This bus station was greatly enlarged again in the early 2000s.

Below: Selfishly parked cars make it very difficult for the driver of RT3480 (BX) to perform a short turn on route 229 at St. Mary Cray Station on 12th May 1977 - he is having to reverse. RMs took over this route nine days later and remained until September 1982.

WAR DAMAGE

London was so badly bombed during the 1940/41 Blitz and again by flying bombs in the closing months of the war that even now, evidence of bomb damage may still be seen. One example is in Essex Road, Islington with a shored up building and a fruit and veg stall occupying the space where the bombed building was remains even today! On 21st May 1967, RT3371 (L) on the 38A, an elderly RT10-bodied vehicle which has just been VERY surprisingly repainted, escorts a Saunders-bodied RT past this site. An Islington Borough Council dustcart completes the picture.

A particularly bad incident during the Blitz was the bombing of St. Thomas's Hospital, Lambeth, in which both nurses and patients were killed. Much of it was left in ruins for long after the war. On 21st February 1968, people watch as the ruins are finally demolished and RT666 (Q) passes on tram replacement route 172. A splendid new hospital was built here in the early 1970s.

Saunders-bodied RT1058 (Q), another on the 172, rounds Highbury Corner on 23rd October 1969. The building behind the RT is a reminder of the "doodlebug" (V1 missile) that fell here at lunchtime on Friday 27th June 1944, demolishing a bank, post office, shops and houses: my mother missed it by just two minutes, her home being just around the corner! The whole area lay in ruins until the roundabout was built in 1958, and a new block of flats, Dixon Clark Court (just out of the picture on the right) added in 1962.

The East End was especially badly hit during the 1940/41, with its docks and factories being targeted by the Luftwaffe. Needless to say houses were hit too, and some of those destroyed here in West India Dock Road, Limehouse have still not been rebuilt as RT1161 (PR) passes on the 277 on 29th August 1973.

London Bridge Station was very badly bombed, especially in May 1941. Wartime damage is finally being rebuilt on 1st February 1974, a cold day judging by how people waiting for their buses are wrapped up. RT4811 (Q), an RM substitution, passes though on route 35.

With unrepaired bombed buildings forming a depressing backdrop, RT3949 (WL) turns from Marshalsea Road into Southwark Bridge Road on 19th March 1976, the last official day of RT working on rush hour route 176A before its RM conversion. This area was also very badly hit during the heavy raid of 10th/11th May 1941.

AT HOME

The difference in width is clearly evident between eight-foot wide RTW143 and RTs 2752 and 2252, just six inches narrower, in Hatfield Country Area garage on 27th April 1968. The latter is one of the Green Line relief RTs, though by now usually used as a Country bus. This garage was opened in 1959 to replace the original building, and was typical of latter-day LT Country Area garages. Sadly, it no longer exists today.

Similarly, the difference in height is obvious between lowbridge RLH68 and standard height RT3584, at home in Hornchurch garage in June 1969. This garage was one of many LT ones closed during the 1980s as a result of losses of routes through tendering to other operators. It closed in 1986.

On 15th February 1970, RT3438 has a Green Line fleet name, but London Transport adverts and radiator badge, despite having passed into London Country ownership at the beginning of the year. It has just run out of Grays Garage to take up service on local route 369.This large, modern garage is also but a memory today.

A driver and conductor are about to take RT4171 out of Seven Kings Garage on route 150 on 7th June 1974. Another busman looks at the rota lists on the noticeboards outside the office on the right. This old London General Omnibus Company garage is undergoing rebuilding, not least because its layout is too restrictive for anything bigger than an RT to negotiate. Therefore at this time, it was the last all-RT garage. Some of them had to be housed in the nearby goods yard at Goodmayes Station while rebuilding took place. It was completed in early 1976, enabling route 86 to convert to RM, and subsequently DMSs also ran from the garage. But all was in vain - this garage too was closed some ten years later.

Above: Routes 176 and 176A were the last to be all-RT operated into the West End and City respectively. A group of them are seen in Walworth Garage, a former tram depot that was substantially rebuilt for bus operation. On their final evening of scheduled RT operation, 19th March 1976. RT3871 and RT4779 are nearest the camera and are preserved today. However, odd RTs would remain at this garage to assist ailing RMs until November 1977. Despite closure in 1985, Walworth later reopened and remains in use today.

Right: Barking was the last London Transport garage of all to operate RTs. At the end, they were parked in the open in the garage yard, where RT1654 and RT2773 face the camera on 9th August 1978, eight months before the end. This garage is also still in use at the time or writing.

LEARNING THE GAME

All bus fleets need their drivers to be trained properly, and London Transport for many years had its famous training school at Chiswick. Usually, older buses withdrawn from public service were kept specifically as trainers. The first RTs to be used for the purpose were the early wartime examples, from the mid-1950s until the early 1960s when they were displaced by RTLs and then RTWs. Post-war RTs in turn displaced these from late 1968 onwards. Euston Tower takes shape on 26th May 1970 as Saunders-bodied RT3809 waits at the traffic lights, advertising Red Rovers which are still seven bob (35p). Use of these roofbox RTs was very short-lived, all had gone by early 1971.

Standard Park Royal or Weymann-bodied RTs comprised most of LT's training fleet throughout most of the 1970s. RT1620 takes a break outside County Hall on 9th November 1975. By coincidence, I had trained as a conductor on this RT in 1974, and had worked in County Hall before and after my time on the buses! The RT contrasts with the ugly DMS about to overtake it, and was later reinstated to public service at Catford Garage.

Towards the end of the RTs' use as driver trainers, many appeared without the familiar "Private" blinds, but not often with empty blind-boxes, as RT2127 has whilst climbing the steep Crouch End Hill on 3rd July 1978!

A shortage of RTs at the same period, when several on training duties had to be returned to service, led to a number of preserved RTs being loaned back to London Transport to make up the numbers. Saunders-bodied RT1320 makes a splendid sight in early postwar Country Area livery as it leaves Chiswick Works on 10th July 1978...but the problem is, no Saunders RT EVER carried green livery when in service! Sadly, such falsities plague the preservation scene even today.

London Country also employed RTs as driver trainers, some of them lasting a few months longer in this role than their LT counterparts. On 30th March 1979, a very battered RT4496 sets off from Windsor Bus Station on a training mission. The RML on the right would soon be sold back to LT and see some 25 years' further service as a red bus!

HILLS

Many parts of London and its surrounding countryside are very hilly, providing a challenge to the RTs that served them, which they did with flying colours. One of the steepest is Muswell Hill, on which Saunders-bodied RT1833 (MH) climbs past the site of the railway station on the Alexandra Palace branch on 20th April 1968. In later years, such types as MBs, DMSs and Metrobuses were often unable to climb this hill in wintry conditions - the RTs and also the RMs managed it with ease!

Working route 133's Sunday extension, which covered both the 43 and 143, on 23rd June 1968, another Saunders, RT1244 (BN), is on the long climb up Archway Road approaching Highgate Station on the Northern Heights. The lack of traffic, apart from a car about to overtake the RT on the A1 Great North Road is striking!

Stag Hill gave a fast run for RTs on routes 29 and 29B then, latterly routes 298 and 299, through the open country on the Hertfordshire/ Greater London borders between Potters Bar and Cockfosters. RT1107 (PB) storms along it on 15th October 1968, shortly after route 298's introduction.

South London has steep hills in the Crystal Palace area. On 6th February 1970, RT3904 (TC) climbs Knights Hill. Norwood Garage is in background - this is the last day of RTs on route 68, and the one in the background is awaiting transfer away from Norwood to nearby Streatham Garage.

The Woolwich area is very hilly too. On 3rd April 1972, RT2804 (TL) works a Sunday trip on the 192, climbing up Griffin Road, Plumstead towards Woodlands Estate. This location is very near Arsenal Football Club's original Invicta football ground, where they played prior moving north of the river to Highbury.

Near to Arsenal's then-current ground at Highbury, RT2294 (B) crests the steep hill up from Blackstock Road to Highbury Park, heading to its home garage on the last day of RT operation on route 19, a route I have known since early childhood, having lived in the area until 1976.

Anerley Hill, like North London's Highgate Hill, is so steep that trolleybuses traversing it had to have special braking to avoid their running backwards out of control in the event of sudden power failures! On 19th April 1973, RT3581 (AL) climbs towards Crystal Palace three weeks before DMSs took over routes 154 and 157. Note the trolleybus traction standard on the left still in use for street lighting. The North Downs may be seen in the distance.

A steep hill always associated with London's trams is Dog Kennel Hill in Duwlich. RT3871 (WL) nears the summit on tram replacement route 176 on 26th February 1976, three weeks before RMs took it over. This RT is now preserved; another is seen further down the hill.

On 26th April 1976 when two rogue RT's had recently been sent to Tottenham Garage to assist ailing RMs, one of them, RT2964 (AR) climbs away from Crouch End Broadway, up Crouch End Hill on busy inner-suburban route 41. The modern Telephone Exchange on the right has today been converted into "luxury apartments"!

Shooters Hill is one of South London's steepest hills, involving a very long climb up to the summit. Recently recertified RT4181 (BX) has almost reached it when seen on 28th April 1976 working the U-shaped route 89, which ran from Lewisham to Eltham via Bexleyheath. RTs would remain on this route for a further two years. Once again, the lack of other traffic here is striking!

Climbing up Farnborough Hill on a scorching hot day, 8th June 1976, RT690 (SP) heads towards its home three days before the RM conversion of route 51. Despite its balding roof this RT saw further service afterwards, notably being sent to Wood Green as an extra spare vehicle to cover for RM shortages in the summer of 1977.

OUT IN THE COUNTRY

Although usually associated with Central London, RTs ran throughout Greater London and also, of course, the London Transport Country Area which extended as far out as forty miles from the city centre. The Buckinghamshire market town of Chesham was typical of such rural outposts served by RTs: on 29th June 1968, RT3335 (MA), another that had originally been red, works the long 335 route to Windsor. It passes RF290 on route 348's terminal stand at Chesham Broadway. RF's, of course, also worked throughout the LT area.

Curiously, many red (Central Area) routes penetrated well beyond Greater London into open countryside. A typical example was those that served the Epping Forest area, and on 3rd May 1969, RT2051 (L) arrives at The Wake Arms in the heart of the forest on a short working of route 20B. This route was RT-operated on Saturdays, with O.P.O. RFs on other days. Six weeks later, it was withdrawn and replaced by an extension of route 20 to Epping upon its conversion to MB operation.

The Bedfordshire town of Luton was another extremity reached by RTs, some of which were based there. On 2nd July 1969, RT3081 (LS) approaches Park Square, Luton, on a short working of route 364, whose through journeys to Hitchin were RF-operated at this time. Luton was the only town served by London Transport that had its own Corporation buses, one of which is seen in the distance. The town was also served by Tilling Group fleet United Counties, which would take over the Corporation's service not long after this picture was taken.

On 27th May 1970, RT3124 (DS) loads up on the long route 414 at Horsham, Carfax - one of the furthest points from Central London in the southern Country Area. Nearly six months after London Country took over these services, the RT still has an LT radiator badge and the bus stop an LT flag - it took a long time to erase traces of some 36 years of LT operation in the former Country Area!

My favourite seat on RTs was the nearside lower-deck one, from which this view of RT3126 (LS) is taken in open country north of Harpenden on 13th July 1972. The long route 321 usually ran in two overlapping sections: Luton to Maple Cross (which these two RTs are on) and St. Albans Garage to Uxbridge. New O.P.O. AN-class Leyland Atlanteans replaced the RTs on this route the day after this picture was taken.

On the same day, 13th July 1972, RT4044 (LS) works the one-bus route 360 and is at its Caddington Village terminus. This was even further out than its base in Luton, buses having to pass beneath the M1 Motorway to Luton's north-west to get there. Despite this, there is still a London Transport bus flag in this small village.

I made the most of a Green Rover ticket, as advertised on RT981(SV) on 13th July 1972, travelling across from Luton to Hitchin on an RF on route 364. Just south of the latter town, another extremity reached by London buses, the RT is seen in the village of Little Wymondley, working one of the Stevenage Industrial Area routes up to Hitchin. Some five and a half years later, this would be the last London Country RT in service bearing original Lincoln green livery. Sadly, it has since been preserved in red - a livery it NEVER carried in service!

The rolling hills of Bourne End, on the long 301 route from Bushey to Aylesbury, form a nice backdrop to this view of a well-filled RT3530 (HH) on 22nd April 1975, shortly before route 301 was converted (in theory, at least) to RMC operation. Unfortunately, an incorrect 302 via blind and a torn destination blind spoil the RT's appearance somewhat.

Down to Downe! Remarkably, one of the most rural London bus routes was the Central Area 146, which ran through country lanes between Hayes (Kent) and the village of Downe. A difficult turn at the latter enforced RTs on the route for many years - at one point it was even considered to paint little GS-class single-deckers in red to replace them! On 29th October 1977, RT2272 (TB) passes Downe Riding Centre - were the horses along this country lane used to seeing RTs thundering along it? Meanwhile, the final solution to the turning problem at Downe was resolved six months later by replacing the RTs by BLs. Route 146 still runs today, being in fact entirely within Greater London.

LANDMARKS

RT2046 (AW) which has just terminated at the Blackfriars end of Victoria Embankment on 11th January 1971 gives an unusual view of St. Paul's Cathedral, behind the war-damaged station buildings. Tram replacement route 171 was subsequently withdrawn from the Embankment loop and cut back to Elephant & Castle.

Part of London County Hall, MY workplace from 1965 to 1974 and again in 1976/77, forms the backdrop for this view of RT2353 (WD), about to terminate at Westminster Station on 15th July 1971. The route converted to DMS the following week.

On 18th December 1971, RT1226 (SW) is framed by the imposing Gothic-style St. Pancras Station and Midland Hotel as it approaches the Kings Cross terminus of weekend route 77C. RM's replaced RTs on the 77 group two years later, and it is remarkable now to think that this imposing building had only recently escaped demolition! The hotel has recently reopened and Eurostar trains from the Continent as well as Midland main line trains terminate here today.

The famous “Big Ben” bell and clock, adjacent to the Houses of Parliament, are actually housed in what was called St. Stephen’s Tower when this view of RT3868 (HT) crossing Westminster Bridge on 22nd September 1972 was taken. The tower has recently been renamed The Elizabeth Tower in honour of Her Majesty Queen Elizabeth II. Tram replacement route 172 retained RTs until August 1975, when crew DMs replaced them.

Tourists crowd at Eros Island down the ‘Dilly as RT1161 (CT), with headlights ablaze, passes through the bus lane leading into Piccadilly itself on 1st September 1976. This was one of two rogue RTs allocated to the busy 38 at the time.

The Elephant & Castle is one of London’s most famous pubs, but the original was destroyed during the May 1941 Blitz. The replacement is the awful glass, steel and concrete structure seen to the offside of RT933 (NX), substituting for an RM on route 141 on 6th February 1974.

More rogue RTs were sent to Holloway and Putney Garages in the autumn of 1976. Working from the latter on a murky 22nd November 1976, RT4631 (AF) is on route 30, which had last been RT-operated in 1955 (and was then worked by RTLs until RM conversion in 1964) at Hyde Park Corner. The Park Lane Hilton looms over The Wellington Arch and entrances to Hyde Park on the left.

HOSPITAL SERVICE

Many "isolation hospitals" and "lunatic asylums" were built on the edge of London, especially in Victorian times. By the 1960s, those still in use often had special bus services, or extensions, in use for those visiting patients. On 29th May 1968, RT3752 (LH) is seen in Epson on special route 472, which ran limited stop to Netherne Hospital only on days when visiting was allowed. The large slipboard in its canopy denotes "protective fares" to avoid short-riders taking up places meant for hospital visitors.

Near Watford Junction on 13th July 1968, RT3892 (GR) works to Holywell Hospital, one of several such establishments in the area. Route 385 had special services for both schools and hospitals!

Special route 808, numbered in the Stevenage New Town "Town Service" series, was actually a limited stop route starting at Chells in the New Town, through which it ran before continuing through the Old Town and along the Great North Road to hospitals in the Hitchin area. On 20th September 1970, RT1296 (SV) calls at "The Pear Tree" on Valley Way in the New Town on the return journey to Chells. For once in this area where there were many confusing blind displays, the blinds are self-explanatory on this RT!

Route 124A was one of few Central Area routes to operate specially for hospitals, in this case on Sunday afternoons to Bexley Mental Hospital. On 4th July 1971, RT4685 (TL) arrives there shortly before the route's (and its parent, the 124) short-lived conversion to RM operation. Since the hospital was on the border of the Central and Country Areas, it was also served by journeys on Country bus route 401 at this time, also with RTs. Unlike many such establishments which in recent years have been closed and converted into "luxury apartments", this one is still open, including a secure unit for convicted murderers with "diminished responsibility".

Banstead was one of the most famous mental hospitals in the London area, served for many years on Sunday afternoons by an extension of route 88, which went right inside the grounds. On 10th September 1972, RT4711 (S) at Charing Cross is very unusually substituting for an RM on a through working from Acton and Central London to the hospital. Such workings ceased in January 1974, Banstead has since been closed and converted for residential use.

Napsbury was another hospital in the Watford area, which had its own limited stop bus service. RT4102 (GR) loads up outside Bushey & Oxhey Station on 29th May 1974. An RT side-blind is fitted in error to its front via box, but at least the correct route details are shown.

Warlingham Park Hospital was the regular terminus of busy route 403, which along with journeys on routes 408 and 470, terminated in the hospital grounds. On 1st May 1976, when route 403 was the last major route to be fully-operated by Country RTs, RT1027 (CM) awaits departure there. The typical LT bus stop (more than six years after LCBS had taken over!) and Country Area shelter on the right are of note.

OUT IN ALL WEATHER

London's RTs had to soldier on through all weathers, through fog, sleet and snow; through the wind and the rain. On a snowy 8th December 1967, Saunders-bodied RT4482 (TH) working route 109 is parked by the roadside at County Hall in the morning rush hour without its driver. Has it come to grief, or been turned short?

The snow had turned to slush the next day, 9th December 1967, on which RT4163 (CM) loads up with passengers at West Croydon Bus Station on Country route 408's long run from Guildford to Chelsham.

In my determination to catch all surviving roofbox RT's on film, I was out in all weather too! On 18th January 1968, the old St. Thomas' Hospital, already badly damaged during the Blitz, is being demolished as Saunders-bodied RT1779 (ED) crosses Westminster Bridge in pouring rain on route 12. It carries an incorrect intermediate blind, meant for short workings of the route between Norwood Junction and South Croydon.

Umbrellas are to the fore as RT4270 (HH), yet another red RT overhauled in green in 1963/64, passes Hemel Hempstead market on local route 314 on 30th March 1968. The people in the foreground appear to be waiting for taxis rather than buses, but the cab rank is empty.

9th May 1968 was another wet day in the Country Area, as RT3362 (LH), also a former red RT, awaits a crew change in Leatherhead town centre. The garage was a few minutes' walk from here, so the crews must have got wet walking to and from it. Route 470 was one of several long Country Area routes that radiated to various towns south of Croydon.

It is pouring with rain on 25th October 1969, too, as Green Line relief RT620 (CM) sploshes through the puddles at Sevenoaks Bus Station on the 403A, which has also come from Croydon. A Maidstone & District A.E.C. Reliance single-decker is just visible on the left - this was "border territory" between that B.E.T. Group fleet and London Transport.

We had a White Christmas in 1970. On Christmas Day, RT3089 (T) calls at the main northbound stops on Islington High Street, with a fair number of passengers aboard. The shops behind it are already advertising their January sales' Route 38 will convert from RT to RM operation on 16th of that month in 1971.

Pouring rain and falling dusk makes an atmospheric shot of the last 244 to run from Archway Station on route 244's rush hour extension. RT3308 (MH) loads up at the foot of Archway Road for the climb up to Highgate and Muswell Hill, and still has pre-1961 upper-case via blinds. SMSs took over this route next day. The 244 was withdrawn in 1982, but today's route 299 covers its section between Muswell Hill and Southgate.

Torrential rain fell in London on 20th July 1972, as RT1377 (NB) stands at the Belmont Station terminus of route 213, a fortnight before its conversion to DMS. This RT was subsequently rescued from a farm near Waltham Abbey by myself and fellow members of the North London Transport Society, then sold for further use as an open-top touring bus on the island of Guernsey, where it still is today!

Unseasonal snow obscured the identity of RT2794 (A) standing at the Morden Station terminus of route 164 on 18th March 1975. The 164 and 164A retained RTs until January 1977 when RMs replaced them.

Below: A few minutes later, the snow had stopped and the sun was out, but RT2085 (A) still has enough covering its blind box at Morden Hall Road roundabout heading south on route 93. This route converted to RM operation, at the end of February 1976.

1976 will always be remembered for its very hot, dry summer. On 26th June 1976, RT732 (E) pauses to pick passengers up in the Hertford Road just south of Waltham Cross, as a group of young ladies enjoy the afternoon sun whilst waiting for a 279. Although the RT has all its side windows wide open, oddly the front upper-deck ones are closed: perhaps they are still locked shut, as buses' front windows were in the winter months?

AROUND AND ABOUT

London's RTs served a wide variety of towns, villages and areas throughout the former Central and Country Areas. A typical suburban centre, where all bus routes were operated by RT-types between 1954 and 1969, was Morden. On 11th November 1967, RT2319 (AL) passes Morden Station, southern terminus of the Northern Line, and three other RTs are also in view. In March 1969, part of this route was replaced by the MBS-type on route M1, whilst routes 80 and 80A were converted to RF and diverted here - thus breaking the RTs' monopoly at Morden.

Showing a slipboard beneath its canopy announcing that minimum fares are charged in the Kingston area where Country route 418 parallels Central Area ones (to protect passengers needing to use this route), RT1700 (LH) runs through Epsom on 29th May 1968. The Kingston to Epsom section of the 418 is still a London buses route today, whilst this RT survives in use on heritage service 339 between Epping and Ongar, as mentioned earlier.

RTs were the backbone of local town services and long-distance trunk routes alike in the Country Area for well over twenty years. On 1st June 1968, a packed RT4563 (GR) is seen in Slough Town Centre heading for its home garage on the long 335 which linked Windsor and Watford.

The 408 was another very long Country Area route, skirting much of the southern edge of the Central Area between Chelsham and Leatherhead before heading out to Guildford. It was also yet another that ran through Croydon. On 5th June 1968, RT3693 (LH) has just crossed the River Mole in Leatherhead and is approaching its home garage.

Two very long Country Area routes linked Croydon and distant Horsham. One was the 414, illustrated previously in these pages, running via Dorking; the other was the 405 which ran via Crawley. On 17th July 1968, RT2153 (CY), another former red RT, passes through Purley Cross on the latter, as a red RT on route 197 turns left behind it bound for Caterham.

At the opposite end of Greater London, RT4083 (E) heads along Lancaster Road, north of Enfield, on local route 128 on 7th June 1969, a week before this route was replaced by flat-fare route W8 with the MBSs. RTs were equally at home working along major trunk roads and suburban residential streets like this.

By 16th April 1970, few roofbox RTs remained in service. They were the last of the line of buses with this typical London feature, which dated back to the late 1920s. Those bodied by Saunders were the last in use, and although the majority had been withdrawn by the summer of 1970, one odd example survived until March 1971 as will be seen later. Here, RT1783 (AP) heads along Ilford Lane on route 193, which had replaced trolleybus route (Barking to Chadwell Heath) in 1959, but was greatly extended to supplement route 86 out to Upminster.

Also in the east of London, new route 294 had been introduced replacing parts of route 66A in July 1970. On 5th September 1970, RT1194 (NS) approaches Romford Station with another RT on route 86 following. It is interesting that all its external advertisements are in-house LT ones.

Route 115 was a curious one, running in a U-shape from Wallington to Purley via Streatham, with a rush hour extension from the latter point to Whyteleafe. A well-filled RT1795 (TH) is in heavy traffic on the Purley Way heading for this destination on 25th September 1970. The route converted to SMS at the beginning of January 1971 and no longer exists today.

"Bunching" is a busmens' term for two or more buses on the same route running together, but surely FIVE RTs in procession on route 49 is ridiculous! This, however, is the case in Broomwood Road, Wandsworth on 13th May 1971, with RT2842 (AK) leading. Two days later, the 49 was cut back from Crystal Palace to Streatham Garage and converted to RM. A new SMS-operated route 249 took over its outer section, paralleling it as far as Clapham Junction.

All is quiet at Grays War Memorial on 11th August 1971, except for a group of people on the left consulting one of town maps that were often to be seen by the roadside in town centres, and an apparently empty RT4192 (GY) working local route 328. It has a side blind in its front via box, and a lazy blind in the side for some reason.

4th March 1972, a busy Saturday at Clapham Junction, finds RT922 (B) working Saturday-only route 39A, which covered the parent 39 between Southfields and Battersea Bridge, from where it replaced the 45 as far as South Kensington Station. This RT, however, wrongly shows a via blind for the 39 running into the West End. Both the 39 and 39A converted to DMS in July 1972.

Route 310 (and the associated 310A) were cross-border Country Area routes that penetrated the Central Area between Waltham Cross and Enfield Town. On 15th April 1972, a smartly repainted RT3631 (HG) turns right from the Great Cambridge Road into Southbury Road. Sadly, this route no longer runs south of Waltham Cross today - indeed there are NO "cross-border" routes there from London into Hertfordshire and Essex as they used to be - it is "all change" at the Bus Station!

Illustrating how private cars were the bane of busmens' lives even in the early 1970s, RT2573 (RD) is trapped amid a line of them in the evening rush hour of 23rd September 1972. It is in Ardleigh Green Road, between Romford and Harold Wood two months before this local route converted to DMS.

Below: On 22nd September 1972, RT3679 (WR) works local route 417 in Slough Town Centre, long after such services here were supposed to have converted to RML (in 1966) and then MBS (in 1969). London Country (and the LT Country Area before it) was much less rigid in its vehicle type-to-route allocations than London Transport, and needed to be when there was a serious vehicle shortage in the mid-1970s. A Country RF and MBS complete the picture.

Above: Shortages of RTs in the autumn of 1972 caused London Transport to re-purchase thirty-four of them from London Country. The buses were merely painted red and pressed into service without overhaul and even in some cases external adverts. This was especially bizarre in the case of RT3232 (BW) as dusk falls on 27th September 1972 at Aldgate East Station. Since new it had worked in the same area as a Green Line coach in 1950, also without external ads and running between Aldgate and Stratford on the 721 and 722 along the same roads it was now serving on route 10! Although the 10 converted to DMS a month later, this RT was to serve LT until July 1978 and is preserved in its original Green Line livery today.

Left: The last tram replacement route to retain RTs was the 155, which finally lost them upon RM conversion in January 1977. That was still in the future when RT3640 (AL) set off from Wimbledon for Elephant & Castle on 11th May 1973.

Route 197 ran along the Caterham Valley to terminate at Caterham-On-The-Hill, but on 28th December 1973, RT1929 (TC) has been unusually curtailed at Whyteleafe. It is beside the railway bridge east of Upper Warlingham Station running around the block to head back to Norwood Junction. DMSs would take over a week later, no doubt causing far more curtailments on the route!

On 1st July 1975, a very well-loaded RT549 (Q) turns from Liverpool Road into Cloudesley Place, Islington, on route 172 in the evening rush hour. This tram replacement route had been diverted away from its original route in Upper Street and the southern end of Holloway Road, in March 1971 to serve Barnsbury. The building behind is the Royal Agricultural Hall, used before the war for various shows but at this time partially used as a G.P.O. sorting office. It has since been resurrected as an exhibition centre. Meanwhile, the 172 was converted to DM a month after this picture was taken and withdrawn from the area seven years later.

Above: Illustrating how versatile RT's were, RT344 (WL) leans over at an apparently precarious angle as it takes St. George's Circus at speed on route 176 in the evening rush hour of 5th March 1976. The buses could in fact lean over far further than this before toppling over, as could be proven by their famous tilt test at Chiswick and Aldenham Works!

Right: The long route 34, running across North London from Barnet to Walthamstow, still runs today and in RT days had many short workings. On 15th July 1976, RT4415 (WW) is at Leyton Green heading for New Southgate, Brunswick Avenue - a rush hour short turn for the benefit of workers at the nearby Standard Telephone Works. DMSs replaced the RTs in September 1977.

RT851 (SP) is full of schoolchildren on route 229 on 12th May 1977, as it keels over turning from Sidcup Station Road into Hatherly Avenue on the long run from Orpington to Woolwich. Nine days later, the route converted to RM but was withdrawn between Erith and Woolwich. That section, on which it had replaced the 698 trolleybus in 1959, was covered by new DMS-operated route 269.

The Barking By-Pass glistens after a summer shower as RT1658 (BK) loads up on the Rainham to Becontree Heath section of route 87 on 9th August 1978. This was the penultimate RT-operated route, converting to RM at the end of October that year.

Route 62 was the last of all to have full RT operation. Also on 9th August 1978, RT2517 (BK) runs on the "country" section of the route, in Billet Lane, Hainault. RMs finally replaced RTs on the 62 on 7th April 1979.

GREENLINE

The first Green Line RTs were a batch delivered to Romford, London Road garage in 1950 for use on routes 721 and 722 which ran from Aldgate to Brentwood and Corbetts Tey respectively. Supposedly coaches, they still had standard RT seating and open platforms, but could be recognised externally by having raised "Green Line" bullseyes between decks on each side, and no external advertisements. More arrived in 1954 for the 723 group of routes running from Aldgate to the Tilbury area. They lasted until the summer of 1965 when they were replaced by new RCL-class Routemaster coaches. On 23rd May 1965, one of the original batch, RT3251 (RE), stands at Aldgate Bus and Coach Station. This RT was bought back by LT in 1972 and lasted until the very last day of RT operation in April 1979. It was then preserved and is now part of the Ensign Heritage Fleet, in red livery.

A number of Country RTs were adorned in Green Line livery in 1960 for use as extras on busy Green Line routes on which the existing, small RFs were having difficulty in coping with demand. They could be distinguished from the original Green Line RTs by having a painted bullseye between decks rather than a raised one. Although larger RMCs replaced RFs on the busiest routes in 1962/63, these RTs were retained for rush hour and bank holiday relief duties. They came in handy in 1967 when the RMCs were having their first overhauls: on a wintry 19th November 1967, RT3607 (SJ) stands in for one on route 717 (Wrotham - Welwyn Garden City) at Golders Green Station. A new waiting room for coach passengers is being built beside it; route 717 reverted to RF operation soon afterwards.

Just as the "relief" Green Line RTs worked indiscriminately on ordinary Country bus routes, so did ordinary Country RTs work on Green Line reliefs! On 25th April 1968, RT4514 (ST) loads up at Hyde Park Corner on route 702 bound for Sunningdale. It has a nicely-set blind display showing it is a Green Line relief.

Almost a year later, on Easter Sunday, 6th April 1969, RT3895(HA) has a good load aboard as it begins to climb Goldings Hill from Loughton into Epping Forest, on route 720 which ran from Aldgate to Bishops Stortford. It is going only as far as its hometown, Harlow.

Next day, Easter Monday 7th April 1969, RT3232 (TG) has arrived at Victoria's Eccleston Bridge Green Line Coach Station (which by now was northbound-only due to a one-way system) to return home to Tring on the usually RF-operated route 706. Many Green Line routes converged here, and on bank holidays relief workings, in the 1960s and 1970s with both RTs and RMLs, were plentiful. This RT is of interest in that it was one of the original Romford Green Line batch, all of which were downgraded to bus status in 1965 and given overhauls as buses in 1968/69. As shown earlier, this one was bought back by LT in 1972.

A typical use for Green Line reliefs was to take spectators to sporting events. On Easter Monday, 3rd April 1972, RT3145 (SJ) is overheating as it arrives at Brands Hatch motor racing circuit with a full load of passengers from London. It has recently been repainted in London Country's new livery of Lincoln green with yellow waistband and signage. Why the destination "West Kingsdown" is shown is anybody's guess!

Framed by the British Overseas Airways Terminal in Buckingham Palace Road, Victoria, on 27th August 1973, the Sunday of August Bank Holiday weekend, Green Line relief RT1106 (ST) has brought a crowd of day-trippers home from Windsor and Hampton Court, both busy tourist spots being served by the 718, on which the RP in front is probably the scheduled vehicle. Interestingly, it ran back as a 701 to Staines, its home town. Its blind display is of course wrong - it was terminating at Eccleston Bridge.

Above: On Whit Monday, 27th May 1974, RT3816 (HA) is also working route 718 as a relief, but along the whole route from Windsor to Harlow. It has a full load aboard when turning off the A3 at Roehampton, Earl Spencer in order to serve Putney. The picture was taken mid-morning, so presumably the passengers are on a day-trip to see London's sights or possibly to ramble through Epping Forest.

Right: A very late appearance in the RTs' lives of one on Green Line work was a scheduled evening rush hour duty from Victoria to Tring on route 706 towards the end of the hot summer of 1976. This resulted from shortages of the SNC-class Leyland Nationals usually used on the route (which had been the last with full RF operation three years previously) which were expiring, probably due to the heat! On 1st September 1976, RT3530 (TG) which has a full blind display rather than a "relief" one, approaches Marble Arch. Its lack of passengers emphasises the drop in patronage of Green Line services by this time.

TOWN SERVICE

Upon the establishment of New Towns in London's suburban countryside after the war, a new series of route numbers for Country buses serving them on local routes was established. Numbers 800 - 849 were allocated to the Northern Country area, and 850 - 899 to the Southern. Fewer were to be used in the latter, mostly at Crawley, and an odd case was the 854, serving Orpington and the small Ramsden Estate on its outskirts. On 3rd September 1966, RT640 (DG) is at Orpington Station. For some reason, the route was renumbered 493 a few months later. Moreover, the route was entirely within Greater London and later became a London Buses (red) route.

Conversely, some Country Area routes numbered in the normal series (300s north, 400s south) became New Town services, often displaying the rather vague "Town Service" lazy via blinds. An example is green ex-red RT1548 (HA) laying over between turns to the nearby bus station at its home garage, Harlow on 6th April 1968, when both RTs and RMLs could be found on route 397.

Other local services in the Country Area which served existing towns rather than New Towns had route numbers in the normal series, and showed lazy via blinds. RT1043 (DS) running through Dorking town centre on 5th June 1968 illustrates this.

Despite having route numbers in the 850 series for local New Town services, others at Crawley were numbered in the normal series. On 5th June 1968, Green Line relief RT3616 (CY) departs from the New Town's bus station for its garage on local route 426A, leaving another RT and an RF behind.

Local town services in the Welwyn Garden City and Hatfield area were all numbered originally in the normal series, as shown on 14th February 1969 by ex-red RT3375 on route 324 calling at The Cherry Tree pub beside the Great Northern main line in Welwyn Garden City. The use of the large via blind to merely show "Town Service", whilst the destination "Knightsfield via Ludwick Way Hernswood Road" is crammed onto the small final blind, is bizarre to say the least! These services were taken over by flat-fare MBSs next day.

Hemel Hempstead's New Town services were numbered in the conventional series, too. Also on Valentine's Day 1969, RT3520 (HH) is in the centre of the New Town and also has a somewhat crammed final blind! Here too, RTs on these routes were replaced next day by MBSs. The displaced RTs were mostly not withdrawn, however, but overhauled in red to replace older roofbox RTs in the Central Area.

Yet again, local services in Slough were numbered in the normal Country Area series. Also due to be replaced by new MBSs next day, RT2157 (WR) has just left Slough Station on 14th March 1969 on route 446 which was also RML-operated. This RT, originally red, survives in that livery today, entrapped between houses in Camden Town for many years in use as an estate agent's office!

With a lazy blind and no separate destination display, RT3738 (ST) has just crossed Staines Bridge working local route 441C on 1st November 1969, just two months before London Transport would lose its Country Area and Green Line services. This route was a variation of the long route 441, which ran all the way to High Wycombe.

Use of lazy via blinds for town services continued well into the London Country era, as displayed by RT1005 (CY) at Crawley Garage on 27th May 1970, accompanying one of the MBSs foisted on this area in the last months of LT operation.

Above: Stevenage New Town had the greatest network of RT-operated town services, originally numbered 392 and 392A prior to a new series starting at 800 being introduced. I remember these very well, having had folks "emigrate" there from Highbury in 1956! The routes evolved into a series of very complicated workings, particularly serving the town's industrial area east of the Great Northern main line. In the evening rush hour of 13th July 1972, RT3192 (SV) is one of three catering for home bound workers there on route 802B in Gunnels Wood Road.

Above: The New Town routes in Stevenage served the Old Town as well, in order to reach the railway station, to where RT2779 (SV) is apparently heading when seen calling at The White Lion pub on the old Great North Road on 10th October 1972, a few days before most of the RTs working these services were replaced by new ANs.

Right: New "town service" routes with numbers in the 800 series were introduced in Harlow New Town quite late in the RTs' lives. On 7th June 1974, RT1700 (HA) heads through the New Town for Harlow Mill Station.

ODD MEN OUT

Despite London Transport's strict "vehicle type to route" policy, especially in the Central Area, RTs inevitably strayed onto routes they were not scheduled to operate. A very rare sight on 7th June 1967 is that of RT3226, an ex-Green Line RT freshly overhauled in red to replace RTLs at Battersea Garage, working route 52 at Victoria Station on loan to nearby Gillingham Street Garage. Route 52 had converted from RTL to RM in the autumn of 1966 and not been officially RT operated since the early 1950s.

Similarly, it was very rare for RTs to work on most trolleybus replacement routes that had been introduced using RMs. On 14th July 1967 at Clapton Pond, RT2707 (WW) works route 257 which had replaced the 557 trolleybus in February 1960. Such workings became possible when an allocation of RTs was given to Walthamstow Garage in 1964 for routes 34 and 144. Route 257 was withdrawn on 7th September 1968.

Country Area route 436, which ran from Guildford to Staines, was well-known for its RLHs, needed owing to low bridges on the route. However, odd short rush hour journeys that did not venture under these were worked by RTs, such as RT3199 (WY) running out from Addlestone Garage past The Duke's Head pub on 9th May 1968.

On 7th May 1970, I was turned to stone by being confronted by RT965 (FY) working route 104 at Highbury Corner as I emerged from Highbury & Islington tube station on the way home from work! Luckily, I always carried a camera in those days, as this was a very rare working indeed. The 104 was the pioneer RML-operated route which had replaced the 609 trolleybus in November 1961. Its garage, Finchley, gained a small allocation of RTs for route 125, but these never usually strayed onto the 104. The most likely explanation is that RM965 was also based at the same garage, and the fitters probably got the two buses mixed up when dressing them for service!

Route 214 replaced the 615 trolleybus route in February 1961, but its operating garage, Highgate, did not receive RTs until late in 1965, therefore, the appearance of their RT1756 (HT) on route 214 on 10th June 1970 is also a rarity. It passes the once-famous Dawson Bros department store at the junction of City Road and East Road. The garage lost its RTs in March 1971, and although many more were moved there when Holloway (J) Garage closed six months later, they did not carry blinds for route 214.

Busy route 409, which ran all the way from West Croydon to Forest Row in Sussex, had been one of the first to convert to RMLs in the Country Area in late 1965, but by 19th April 1973, when RT3450 (GD) was heading south along Croydon High Street, there was a shortage of RMLs, obliging RTs to be used to cover for them. In this view, an SMS follows on route 12A.

Similarly, former coach Routemasters of the RCL and RMC classes based at Grays for the busy 370 were in short supply too at this period, also meaning the return of RTs. RT603 (GY) has just passed Romford Station on 4th August 1973 and has an Routemaster side-blind in its front via box.

Swanley's RMC's were also thin on the ground, therefore RT4740 has come to the rescue on route 477. It leaves Orpington Station on 18th Semptember 1973 sporting a decidedly odd front blind display, and behind it is the then-current generation of buses - an SM and a Leyland National. None of these would last anywhere near as long as the faithful RTs!

By the end of 1973, a nationwide shortage of spare parts for buses had really begun to bite. RM-types were particularly badly affected, and London Transport was forced to send spare RTs to cover for missing RMs at garages that had not operated them for years. The first was RT3925 (AR), sent to Tottenham Garage. It is in Black Boy Lane, West Green on route 171 on 29th December 1973. Tottenham had only had a full allocation of RTs for this route between 15th June 1968 (when they replaced RTLs) until 7th September that year, when it converted to RM. Hitherto, the garage had operated RTLs and RTWs since the early 1950s, and not usually RTs.

On 15th February 1974, RT489 (AR) was one of three helping out RM shortages at Tottenham, and has very rarely been put in service on the busy 73, which was one of the first routes to convert from RT-types to RM, back in December 1962. It is seen stuck in traffic in Kensington Gore and like the other two RTs at the garage, had RM side-blinds fitted to its front via box, with masking to obscure the fact that they did not fit properly. These RTs moved away in the spring, but others would be back two years later!

On 30th December 1974 another case of an RT covering for RMs on a trolleybus replacement route is that of RT4411 (R) on route 266. This too was a very rare working. Its conductor consults his driver in Acton Vale, where shops advertise their winter sales. The RT is from Riverside Garage, Hammersmith, which had a small share of the route at the time, and is from their allocation for route 72. This converted to RM a year later, putting an end to such workings.

RT1641 (R) is also a Riverside bus, and on 18th September 1975 finds itself on an extremely rare working, covering for an RML on weekday route 74B (Camden Town - Hammersmith via Earls Court) which had been introduced with RTWs and then converted to Routemaster operation, never having been scheduled for RTs. The bus passes the Victoria & Albert Museum with a standing load and is on a short working to Earls Court.

Following the introduction of new route 217B (with RTs) at Ponders End Garage in April 1976, all RMs and RTs at the garage had new blinds, which were compatible for them working all of each other's routes. Thus for the first time, RTs could be seen substituting for RMs on trolleybus replacement route 279. On 26th April 1976, exactly fifteen years after its introduction, RT4316 (E) performs a U-turn on a short working to Manor House. This view nicely shows the nearside profile of a standard RT. Today, route 279 terminates here daily, still doing a U-turn across the busy main road.

History repeated itself in the spring of 1976, when two rogue RTs were sent to Tottenham Garage to help with RM shortages. Also on 26th April 1976, presumably by coincidence, both - RT2178 and RT2964 (AR) - were running together on route 41 and stand side by side at its Tottenham Hale Station terminus. A third RT was added at the garage a few months later.

Route 76 was also graced by Tottenham's rogue RTs, and in the evening rush hour of 29th April 1976, RT2178 (AR) is at the junction of East Road and New North Road, Hoxton escorting a National Express Bristol RELH coach and an RM. Ten years before, route 76's RTWs had been replaced firstly by new RMLs and then by XA-class Leyland Atlanteans in trials to establish which of the two types performed best: needless to say, the RMLs won!

During the winter of 1975/76, local Croydon area route 190 had been operated by a batch of Southend Corporation Leyland PD3 Titans on loan to LT in order to alleviate a shortage of RMs. These returned in the spring of 1976, but a solitary rogue RT was also sent to South Croydon Garage and used on the route. On 21st May 1976, RT4154 (TC), complete with a clumsily masked RM front via blind, passes beneath the Southern Region main lines in Marlpit Lane, Coulsdon on its climb towards Old Coulsdon. It was there for only a few weeks.

Much to my outrage, since I had until recently worked as a conductor solely on RMs at Clapton Garage, two RTs were sent there in May 1976 and put to work on the busy 38. One of these, RT1706 (CT), was fully repainted and is seen leaving the bus lane through Eros Island down the 'Dilly on 15th June 1976. The 38 had used some of the very first post-war RTs (from Leyton Garage) in May 1947, and converted to RM in January 1971.

Country route 406 had received RMCs early in 1973, but the hot, dry summer of 1976 added to their woes and RTs continued to be used on the route. In Brook Street, Kingston RT3450 (LH) has its windscreen windows wide open, a sight not often seen, as it heads for Tadworth on a short working on a very hot 3rd July 1976. An SM follows on route 418.

RMLs at Staines Garage were also falling by the wayside thick and fast at this period leading to RTs having to cover for them, too. In the evening rush hour of 14th July 1976, RT3607(ST) loads up in Clarence Street, Staines on local route 469 and has an incorrect canopy blind!

The hot summer of 1976 exacerbated existing problems with vehicle shortages, not least with the DMSs overheating and catching fire! RM-types often had to cover for crew DMs, resulting in more RTs being drafted in to RM garages to cover for them in turn. At the beginning of August, no fewer than six RTs were sent to Gillingham Street, Victoria Garage, which had not had a regular RT allocation for well over twenty years, for route 137. One of these, RT3816 (GM) turns from Euston Road into Hampstead Road on the evening of 19th August 1976. These RTs remained on the route well into the spring of 1977.

RTs at garages where RTs and RMs were both allocated normally at this time were often supplemented by extra ones, meaning that RTs operating on routes normally using RMs became more common. An example of this is RT2775 (AD), ostensibly allocated to Palmers Green for routes 34, 102 and 261, working route 298A (and wrongly showing the number 298!) at Palmers Green Triangle on 15th October 1976. The idiot in the car parked on the bus stop has forced it to pick up and set down passengers in the middle of Green Lanes!

RMCs in the northern part of London Country's area were plagued by shortages of spare parts too, meaning that RT4792 (HG) has had to cover for them on busy route 341. It is in St. Peter's Street, St. Albans, also on 16th October 1976. Only a year later, the RMCs on this route were replaced by Leyland Nationals.

A surprise at the beginning of November 1976 was the appearance of two RTs at Wood Green Garage. I varied my journey from Wood Green to County Hall by travelling aboard RT280 (WN) on route 141 to Moorgate, where it has terminated on 4th November 1976, and then continuing by 76 - arriving about half an hour late at the office! The two RTs transferred to route 29 in March 1977, being joined later by a third one.

Two rogue RTs were also sent to Finchley Garage at the beginning of August 1976, and used on route 26 (New Barnet - Victoria via Golders Green), which had been introduced with RMs in June 1970 and had never been RT-operated. Originally, both had just handwritten route numbers in their front and side via boxes, but later RM rear number blinds were used, as seen on RT2143 loading up at North Finchley Tally Ho! Bus Station. Such offside loading would be frowned upon today. This bus station, opened originally for trolleybuses in the 1930s, no longer exists.

Leyton-worked route 230 (Manor House - Stratford) was converted entirely from RM to RT operation in December 1976. The RTs were given neatly masked RM front via blinds. RT2554 (T) is at Seven Sisters Station (Ward's Corner) on 3rd September 1977, shortly before the RMs returned to the route.

By 28th September 1977, many of the rogue RT allocations had ceased, but those that had been allocated to Holloway Garage in the autumn of 1976 continued to surprise us! Most outrageously of all, RT2352 (HT) was pressed into service that day on then-normally crew DM-operated route 104. In the evening rush hour, the small 56-seater has had to leave several passengers behind in Islington High Street as an RM passes on route 171. Usually, the rogue RTs at Holloway worked routes 14, 19 and 27, as well as the 29 after that route reverted to RM operation in March 1977. This was only the second (and last) time that an RT ever worked route 104, and by chance I caught both on film!

Putney Garage had also received a number of rogue RTs in the autumn of 1976 and they worked routes 14, 30 and 74 covering for RMs and RMLs. They were moved away in the spring of 1977, but Holloway RTs still appeared on route 14 well into the autumn - a very smart RT3911, in contrast to the others which were mostly shabby, sloshes through the rain along Euston Road on 20th October 1977. By the end of that year, the last unscheduled allocations of RTs to non-RT garages had finally ceased.

Even in the RTs' final year, however, they were still used to substitute for RMs on routes that had had that type for some years. On 26th July 1978. RT449 (TB) leaves Bromley Garage on route 47, a month before RT working in South London ceased. RTs on this route from both Bromley and Catford garages were the last to work through the City of London.

Local route 119 was also graced by Bromley RTs until the end. Also on 26th July 1978, RT714 (TB) is working it on Corkscrew Hill, West Wickham, where in less pleasant weather, passengers sometimes had to alight and help push the RTs up the hill in the snow!

RTs substituting for RMs from Catford Garage on route 1 had the dubious distinction of being the last ever to work through London's West End. On 23rd August 1978, in the last week of operation, RT4210 (TL) has done so but now passes the awful 1960s housing south of Elephant & Castle.

THE ODD SPOT

In addition to odd workings, there were routes operated for special occasions that RTs worked, routes diverted away from their usual streets for various reasons, and also some RTs that were odd in themselves. One that certainly was odd was RT2776. This had travelled to the U.S.A. promoting Britain when new in 1952, and was given extra ventilation above its front upper-deck windows. It was nicknamed "the eyebrows RT" as a result and retained its original body until its last overhaul. Here it bounces over the cobbles at Stratford Broadway working route 86 from Upton Park Garage on 14th July 1967. Sadly, the body was last overhauled on RT1708 early in 1969, and eventually scrapped.

RTs often operated special routes for sporting occasions, the most famous being route 406F from Epsom Station to the racecourse on the downs. RTs from all over the Country Area were brought to operate it on Derby Day - on 29th May 1968, RT1029 (NF) heads a line-up of eight RTs waiting for passengers at Epsom Station and has come from Northfleet. The conductor on the right already looks tired, and it is only lunchtime!

A lesser-known RT oddity was Country RT3081 (LS) which is loading up on the long 321 route in St. Peter's Street, St. Albans on 14th February 1969. One of several red and green RTs overhauled in the summer of 1966 with white fleetnames rather than the usual gold ones, it also uniquely had a light green waistband instead of a cream one. This was given to Green Line RTs, but not upon overhaul to Country buses. When subsequently Green Line RTs were downgraded to bus status, they retained these causing some people to think this RT had originally been one. It never was a Green Line RT and in fact was originally red!

The Biggin Hill Air Show also produced RTs working extras on route 410 to and from the aerodrome and Bromley North Station. Once again, RTs came from garages other than those usually working the route - On 20th September 1969 at Bromley Market, RT3610 (GY) has come from Grays. Red RTs were also sometimes borrowed for this service, as happened on this occasion - for the last time, as Country Area services were lost to the National Bus Company on 1st January 1970.

On Sunday 9th May 1971, Arsenal Football Club are celebrating winning "the double", both the FA Cup and the League, and parading along Upper Street to a reception at Islington Town Hall. Therefore, buses usually traversing that main road were diverted along Canonbury Road. Here RT2028 (J) escorts another RT on route 19 past an old block of flats called Canonbury Avenue, which was my home until July 1973.

Things are not as they seem in this view of RT4802 (Q) apparently working route 172 on 25th October 1971. It has in fact been used for a mechanics' call-out to a failed MBA on the approach road to Waterloo Station. Note the special bus stop for Red Arrow 503 between the two vehicles. These vehicles lasted twelve years at best; some RTs ran for more than thirty years. That says it all, really!

Construction of a bridge linking County Hall's South Block with the monstrous Island Block built in the middle of Addington Street roundabout caused buses heading south off Westminster Bridge to be diverted through the forecourt of County Hall one weekend in June 1972. On 25th June 1972, RT2388 (AL) turns right from the forecourt into Chicheley Street, from where it will turn right again into York Road, then left into Addington Street to regain the correct line of weekend route for the 77C.

Serious road subsidence in Lee High Road in the early 1970s caused buses on several routes traversing it (all RT-operated at the time) to be diverted southbound via Belmont Hill and Brandram Road. The latter was a quiet residential street, whose inhabitants were outraged at buses thundering past their houses! On 18th November 1972, RT2875 (NX) does so on the first day of operation of new route 151, introduced to serve the new Ferrier Estate at Kidbrooke. This was the last time a new Central Area RT-operated route was given lazy blinds.

Rioting in Brixton and consequent damage to shops and road infrastructure caused diversions of northbound buses through the area in December 1972. On 12th December 1972, RT1808 (TH) is one of two 109's turning from Caldwell Street into Clapham Road, Kennington on this diversion. Much worse riots took place in Brixton in April 1981, but by then, the RTs had gone!

RTs were often used to cover rail replacement services for both the London Underground and British Railways. For the latter, a substantial fleet of London Country RTs ran from Hertford Garage in the spring of 1973 replacing trains on the Great Northern Hertford Loop between Cuffley and Hertford whilst Ponsbourne Tunnel was being rebuilt to take overhead wiring for the line's electrification. The RTs traversed country lanes usually served only by single-deckers on route 308. Two of them, RT4550 and RT3252 (HG) are awaiting passengers at Cuffley Station on 26th April 1973.

Whit Monday, 26th May 1975, saw several RTs running Bank Holiday extras on route 65, which served both Kew Gardens and Chessington Zoo. RT4412 (NB) is heading for the latter when seen unusually turning short in the scenic setting of Kew Green. As so often, stupid motorists have parked cars obstructing the bus' path, to a stand often used by short-working No.27's. This was one of the last occasions red RTs worked such Bank Holiday extras, as the 65 converted to RM the following October.

ALDENHAM

It was largely thanks to the excellent in-house overhaul facilities London Transport had at Chiswick and Aldenham Works that the RTs ran successfully for so many years. Their bodies were overhauled at Aldenham and were almost as good as new when outshopped. Both Works also had a fleet of staff buses to take workers to and from all parts of the London Transport area. These were usually retired service buses, like early 3RT3 RT337 which was the Watford staff bus. It is on Elstree Hill on 11th July 1967.

Left: When Aldenham Works opened fully for bus overhauling in the mid-1950s, delivery of the RT family of buses had recently ended. Because their bodies took a few days longer to overhaul than their mechanical parts, most buses exchanged bodies at overhaul and fifteen extra RT bodies were built to avoid any shortages. These were eventually absorbed into the overhaul system, whilst on the other hand others were kept as "floats", sometimes in later years being used to replace bodies badly damaged in accidents. On 9th November 1967, a group of spare RT bodies were still on the float rack outside the works. The one nearest the camera had last been carried by RT1558.

Below: Also at Aldenham on 9th November 1967, the body from RT1804 which had been involved in a serious collision resulting in the bus half-demolishing a shop accompanies that of RTL70, which was also damaged beyond repair. Both are on the float rack and can be used as a source of spare parts. RT1804 was returned to service with a body from the overhaul system.

During the early to late 1960s, most staff buses were RTLs, but during 1969, a number of Country RTs with early RT3/1 bodies, which had been overhauled green ex-red in 1963/64, were appropriated for use as staff buses. They remained in green livery after the Country Area was lost to LT, as shown by the Hackney staff bus, RT2729, leaving Aldenham on 26th May 1970. All however were withdrawn shortly after this, replaced by newer red RTs.

A peep through the perimeter fence at Aldenham on 4th October 1972 at RT2374, sent there for recertification, gives some idea how huge the Works buildings were - and this is only in fact a small part of them! The building was originally intended as a depot for the Northern Line, on its new extension beyond Edgware to Bushey Heath, which was abandoned due to World War Two. As for RT2374, it saw another two years' service at Barking and Seven Kings Garages after this!

Above: Inside the Works on the same day, RT3822 is one of several RTs which have had three-year recertifications and repaints (in effect a minor overhaul) during the year as a result of the need to keep RTs going owing to the failure of the DMS class, of which a new delivery is seen on the left. A newly-overhauled RM completes the picture. RTs continued to be repainted for further use until as late as early 1978.

Right: In complete contrast, these four withdrawn RTs at the rear of Aldenham Works on 12th May 1977 are being used as seat stores for the type. They are RT3496, 4646, 795 and 4422. The latter on the extreme right of the picture had only recently been withdrawn.

RT staff buses still lingered on at Aldenham until almost the end of RT operation. On 2nd November 1978, RT1907 carries a very incompatible set of blinds and is in fact used for short runs to and from nearby Borehamwood, though officially based at Holloway. The other RT is RT2750, which had been repainted only in March 1978 and sent to Barking garage, where it was withdrawn when route 87 converted to RM operation just five days before this picture was taken.

LAST SURVIVORS

Inevitably, odd variants of the RT family survived longer than others for various reasons. The most bizarre was service vehicle 1037J, which carried the prototype RT body fitted to RT1 in 1939 but was married up to the chassis of post-war RT1420 (one of the Cravens batch) in 1955 after the latter's non-standard body had been wrecked in a low bridge accident. It was used as a mobile instruction unit for bus mechanics, and languished in West Ham Garage for many years. It is seen there on 21st April 1968, and illustrates how this and the wartime 2RT2s had a roof route-number box on the rear as well as the front. It is unfortunate that this historic body was not preserved officially by London Transport, for although the vehicle was eventually rescued, it was restored masquerading as "RT1", which it certainly is not, and still does today!

A standard wartime 2RT2 which survived for many years was another service vehicle, turnover vehicle 1036TV, originally RT106, converted as such when these buses were withdrawn from public service in 1955. It was used to train emergency crews in the raising of overturned buses and ended its days in the yard of Stonebridge Park Garage as a target for the many vandals infesting that area. It's in the yard on 18th October 1970, shortly before going for scrap. What a shame the chassis of this vehicle could not have been married up with the body of RT1, though the body mountings for the latter were not entirely compatible with it.

Although the last examples of the first type of postwar RT, the 3RT3, were withdrawn early in 1965, for some reason a handful of them were kept on as staff buses based at Country Area garages for another four or five years. One of these, RT329, is in the yard of Tring Garage on 29th June 1968. It was later preserved.

The last roofbox RTs in public service in London were those bodied by Saunders. They were last overhauled in 1965/66, by now with stocknumbers throughout the red RT fleet. Most were withdrawn by the summer of 1970, but one odd one, RT1903, had been fitted with saloon heaters on overhaul, apparently in error as only newer RT bodies were meant to have them. It therefore outlived the others, and in the evening rush hour of 2nd March 1971 it is at Holborn Statio.n most unusually working from Battersea Garage substituting for an RM on route 22. Sadly, only a day or two after this picture was taken it suffered rear-end damage, so was withdrawn anyway.

One of the earlier RT10-bodied roofbox RTs (whose bodies were also able to be fitted to RTLs whereas RT3 type and Saunders ones could not), RT4325, survived long after the last was withdrawn from public service in February 1970. At first used as a mobile classroom to teach crews the pleasures of decimalisation, it later become a radio training unit. On 14th September 1973, shortly before its final withdrawal, it runs along Euston Road.

As mentioned earlier, three London Country service RTs were painted in standard NBC livery in the spring of 1977, in addition to two driver trainers already so painted. They did not last long, however, and the last in service was RT604. It is near Fairfield Halls in Croydon on route 403 on 19th April 1978, shortly before withdrawal. It was later used as a trainer and is splendidly restored in this livery today.

The last RT route in North London was the 140 - ironic, since LT had originally intended to convert it to RM in the summer of 1962! On its last day, 14th July 1978, RT3234 (HD) leaves Harrow Weald Garage suitably bedecked for the final run.

Below: Six weeks later, the last RTs ran in South London from Catford and Bromley Garages on route 94 (along with a few RM subs on routes 1, 47, 119 and 180). On their last day, 26th August 1978, RT2146 is also suitably bedecked at Petts Wood Station.

As is well known, route 62 at Barking was the last RT-operated London route of all, its conversion to RM delayed by awkward clearances on the bridge over the Great Eastern main line at Chadwell Hill Station. On 7th April 1979, the last one, RT624 (BK) prepares to set off from Gascoigne Estate for the last run back to the garage. The lack of decoration for this last journey is most noticeable! Afterwards, a farewell cavalcade of RTs ran over the route and back, and this RT is now preserved.

For some while after the last ran in public service, a few London Transport RTs still soldiered on as driver trainers. But the very last was withdrawn on 31st December 1979. By a remarkable coincidence I was visiting an RT that I co-owned kept at the Woolwich Industrial Estate that day, and this last one - RT4566 (AM) - appeared, taken out for a final spin from Plumstead Garage. Dusk falls on the last day of the 1970s, as the RT which has lost its bonnet plate pulls out of Nathan Way to run back home for the very last time.

Even the withdrawal of training RTs was not quite the end. Two of them, RT2143 and RT1530, were kept at Chiswick Works for a few more months as skid buses, testing trainee drivers' wits on slippery surfaces. They await another spin in May 1980.

Another late survivor in the LT fleet, officially a radio trainer, was RT2958. It is outside the new Plumstead Garage on the day it opened in October 1981, and has been used to bring publicity for the changes to bus services in the area which resulted.

END OF THE ROAD

General withdrawal of RTs began once the last RTLs had been withdrawn at the end of November 1968. The first to go were the surviving roofbox vehicles, and on 22nd March 1969, RT1035, 2471 and 4398, all Saunders-bodied vehicles, await disposal at the rear of Bexleyheath Garage along with RTLs, such as RTL121 on the right, which had been there since June 1968. Most, if not all, went for scrap.

Inevitably, RTs became surplus to requirements when newer types replaced them, especially once one-person-operation became all the rage from the late 1960s onwards. On 11th August 1971, a group of London Country RTs with RT4761 nearest the camera await disposal in Grays Garage, following replacement by new SM types. Most went for scrap.

Sadly, most RTs ended up like this in the later years, reduced to skeletons at Wombwell Diesels near Barnsley and burnt, after re-usable parts and metal had been removed. These remains were photographed there on 5th July 1979. What would preservationists give for those seats left in the nearest skeleton today?

Bexleyheath, Poplar, Kingston and Stonebridge Park Garages were the concentration points for withdrawn London Transport RTs in their final years, when few people wanted them and these too mostly went for scrap. On 8th January 1978, RT4034 makes a sad sight dumped at the latter - it is at least interesting to see that the SMS in front of it, which was only six or seven years old, is also due for the chop!

But it was not quite all doom and gloom: of these complete RTs at Wombwell on 5th July 1979, RT3254 on the extreme left of this picture and RT2150, third from left, were both rescued for preservation and survive today!

GARAGE CODES

The Key To Garages Mentioned In This Book:

1. CENTRAL AREA (red buses):

A - Sutton
AB - Twickenham
AC - Willesden
AD - Palmers Green
AE - Hendon
AF - Putney (Chelverton Road)
AK - Streatham
AL - Merton
AM - Plumstead
AP - Seven Kings
AR - Tottenham
AV - Hounslow
AW - Abbey Wood
B - Battersea
BK - Barking
BN - Brixton
BW - Bow
BX - Bexleyheath
CF - Chalk Farm
CT - Clapton
D - Dalston
E - Enfield (Ponders End)
ED - Elmers End
EW - Edgware
FY - Finchley
GM - Gillingham Street (Victoria)
H - Hackney
HD - Harrow Weald
HT - Highgate (renamed Holloway, 9/71)
HW - Southall
J - Holloway
K - Kingston
L - Loughton
MH - Muswell Hill
N - Norwood
NB - Norbiton
NS - North Street (Romford)
NX - New Cross
ON - Alperton
PB - Potters Bar
PM - Peckham
Q - Camberwell
R - Riverside
RD - Hornchurch
RL - Rye Lane, Peckham
S - Shepherds Bush
SE - Stonebridge
SP - Sidcup
SW - Stockwell
T - Leyton
TB - Bromley
TC - Croydon
TH - Thornton Heath
TL - Catford
U - Upton Park
UX - Uxbridge
V - Turnham Green
W - Cricklewood
WD - Wandsworth
WH - West Ham
WL - Walworth
WN - Wood Green
WW - Walthamstow
X - Middle Row, North Kensington

2. COUNTRY AREA (green buses & Green Line coaches)

CM - Chelsham
CY - Crawley
DG - Dunton Green
DS - Dorking
DT - Dartford
EG - East Grinstead
GD - Godstone
GF - Guildford
GR - Garston
GY - Grays
HA - Harlow
HE - High Wycombe
HF - Hatfield
HG - Hertford
HH - Hemel Hempstead
LS - Luton
MA - Amersham
NF - Northfleet
RE - Romford (London Road)
RG - Reigate
SA - St. Albans
SJ - Swanley
ST - Staines
SV - Stevenage
TG - Tring
WR - Windsor
WY - Addlestone